NOT
OF
THIS
WORLD

Not of This World

Printed in the United States of America

ISBN 978-0-6155-4755-8

Williams, Dr. Joseph L.

Not of This World

1. Religious. 2. Christian. 3. Spiritual.

DISCLAIMER

This book includes information from many sources and gathered from many personal experiences. It is published for general reference and is not intended to be a substitute for independent verification by readers when necessary and appropriate. The book is sold with the understanding that neither the author nor publisher is engaged in rendering any legal, psychological or accounting advice. The publisher and author disclaim any personal liability, directly or indirectly, for advice or information presented within. Although the author and publisher have prepared this manuscript with utmost care and diligence and have made every effort to ensure the accuracy and completeness of the information contained therein, we assume no responsibility for errors, inaccuracies, omissions or inconsistencies.
Cover Design and Layout: Jason Phillips jasonphillipstudio.com
Author Photo: Reggie Anderson Photographer www.reggiephotos4u.com
For information or to purchase bulk copies of this book, contact:

PO Box 1971
Hiram, GA 30141
404-482-0373

Dedication

Every plant starts its life as a seed. This book you are preparing to read is a flower that comes forth from the seed that my father planted within me.

I dedicate this book to not only my dad, but my friend, my teacher and my protector. Dad I love you, and I honor you in all that I do.

Your son,
Joe

Acknowledgements

My God

Without God, nothing is possible. I am totally sold out for my Lord and Savior Jesus Christ! God thank you for what you have given me. I will use my gifts and talents to bring light to all places where I find darkness! Amen

My Mother

I want to thank my mother for the guidance, love and care that she has always given me. Mom you believed in me when no one else did. You saw something in me before anyone else realized it was there. I love you and thank you for all you have done!

My Ace

Batman had Robin, Bonnie had Clyde and I have Mrs. Stephania Andry! Steph, you have been there since day one. When all others called me weird and strange, you saw something in me that caused you to feel that others needed to be exposed to it. Many of the things I now know I posses is there because you have helped to polish me into the person that I am. Because of you I am a better person, pastor, writer, radio host and minister to those who are in need. Wherever I go in life, it's my hope that you journey there with me! We have been a great team that has worked on positively changing the lives of many people!

My Support System

There are so many people in and around my life who have made great contributions to me being where I am today. Their love and support have been instrumental in this process. Thank you guys for being there for me—I love you all!

My Team

I want to thank the great and talented team who assisted me with this process. I would like to thank Toni V. Martin, Jason Phillips, Emiene Wright for all they did to make this project a success! I would also like to thank Ms. Rebecca Franklin for her love and support. I look forward to all we will experience together while on this journey!

Table of Contents

Introduction

At the moment of your conception, there was a purpose for you that had been determined before that miraculous event had even occurred. You were made to be something much bigger than any job, relationship or accomplishment you could ever obtain or fulfill.

Just because we are destined to be something bigger than what we see and know doesn't mean that it always happens. So many times, people along the way become distracted, lost and consumed with the darkness of this world. We were all created and made from the light; however, there are times when we are not existing within our home.

The absence of the light creates issues for all for those who attempt to exist without it. Whenever you do not live in the light, it alters your emotional and spiritual states of consciousness. When your state is altered, you will subconsciously reach for inauthentic fillers that leave you in a continual state of misery, pain and depression.

Addictive behaviors will often times exist as a result of these choices and actions. Sexual promiscuity, drug and alcohol abuse will become normal responses of this state. Addictive behaviors exist not because the person is addicted to the act or the substance, but rather because they become addicted to the temporary bliss or numbness the substance or action provides.

What you really desire are the manifestations of the light: joy, happiness, love and peace. You're looking for this state because it is the place where all of us are formed. Just as a child reaches for the sustenance of its mother, we all reach to exist within the realm of that light.

The darkness is not a place that we consciously desire to visit and reside within; however, it is a place where many people are trapped and unable to break free. Humankind has done its best to address the darkness that imprisons us. We have created things such as religion, which will point the reader in the direction of the light.

So what is the light? The light is God, the Supreme Being, the unlimited source of power that creates and sustains all things. When you look at the sun, you see a core and if you look around its perimeter you will see rays. The rays are made from the same elements as the core. The light or God is that core; all other things are extensions of that.

Evil does not exist because the nature of humankind is evil; humankind was created in the image of God. We were all created in the image of the light, extensions of the sun; we were made from love because God is love. It is impossible for a branch of a cherry tree to be anything but a cherry tree. Being that all things are extensions of the light, the light is within us. Evil exists only when that light is unable to shine through the consciousness of that person. When a person is shown how to remove the darkness from their lives in order that they may walk and exist within the light, the darkness will leave as well as all other negative things that accompany it: addictions, anger, hate, jealousy, division etc. They all leave because the authentic self comes through.

When the darkness is removed, the person does not change, they merely become who and what they have always been. When we mine gold from the ground, it's nothing new. The dirt simply has been removed so that what has been there all along may be seen.

There are many powerful elements in religion that are helpful to humankind, but we must understand that the books of religion will only be effective when the story becomes unique to our own personal journey. Religion points humankind in the direction of the light; however, you must find it! This means your journey may start with a book of religious principles, but those uniform principles must turn into an individual spiritual journey. Your journey and my journey may not look alike, but we will experience similar obstacles and joys along the way!

This book is a map and guide that will help you on your journey! It is based on my journey and I have shared it with you in order to assist you on yours! My story is perhaps much like yours. I was once a prisoner of my emotions. I was a prisoner of anger, jealousy and envy. Being a Christian, I always knew I should not have felt as I did; however, I didn't know how to control it.

I am a Christian and I fully accept the life and legacy of Jesus Christ. I wanted to live my life like Christ, but something prevented me from doing that. I didn't understand why I did what I did and thought what I thought or desired the things that I desired. I was a hypocrite, walking around living as if I knew and loved Christ, but my actions were not lining up with what I believed.

I had to change. I had to take the words of God and apply them to my life in a way that caused me to authentically live as Christ did. Today, I can say I have been able to do that. I am pastor to a church of over 10,000 people. I have a radio show that reaches thousands each and every week. I have been able to create different programs in order that people may be set free from the darkness! My message is no different than what I have learned from the life of Christ. I simply tell my story of how that message has changed me!

Because of my journey, I have become a better Christian, person, man, pastor and friend. Every element of my life has changed and I promise you if you follow me on this journey yours will as well.

I did not write this book for a specific group, race, and ethnicity or demographic, I wrote it for all people who desire to change where they are. I wrote it for people who desire to be something better than what they are, though something prevents them from reaching that goal.

Christians, non-believers, Muslims, straight, gay, Republican and Democrats can grow from this book. It is conveyed in a universal language, which is the language of the soul. When you address the soul, you are able to transcend culture, religion, race, gender, socio-economic status, sexual orientation and all other social constructions of humankind.

My story will show that the key to moving from where you are to the path of the light is what I call "The Journey." It is the intentional path those who choose to go there take in order that their lives may be changed forever.

On your journey to the light, you will experience four major stages of change. The four stages are Healing, Transformation, Empowerment and Expansion.

Healing

The first step on your way to the light is the process of being healed. So many are living life as spiritually broken, sick and depressed human beings. Our personalities have been formed by pain and unfortunate circumstances. We live our crippled lives making statements such as, "This is just who I am." These statements cause us to subconsciously accept our position; therefore, we never see the necessity of change.

Depression, abuse, anger and pride are destroying us from within. They shape our personalities until we act in ways that are the complete antithesis of who we are authentically! When you take this journey, the first step you make will be to heal from your past and present state of being. You will heal from the wounds caused in your youth, childhood, and from your past relationships. This step can often be painful and uncomfortable because you will be forced to address issues that you have subconsciously avoided for all this time. Look upon this step as the doorway to the house. The only way to enter the house is through the front door. This book will help you make that first step!

Transformation

The second step of the journey is the process of being transformed. When a caterpillar enters a cocoon and exits as a butterfly, the process is a type of transformation. Things that are transformed are things that are changed. On the second step of the journey, you will be transformed. The transformation is not a physical one, but rather a spiritual one.

Healing and transformation may seem to be similar; however, they are quite separate processes. Healing simply means the wounds that have been caused by the past are dealt with and cared for. Even though a person tends to a wound, the scars don't leave immediately. If someone punches you in the face, they can apologize but the bruise is still there. Just because you are in the process of healing doesn't mean the wounds and effects of what you have experienced immediately disappear, either.

Transformation in your life occurs because you gain an understanding as to how living in the darkness has affected your life. You will understand why you think the things that you think, do the things that you do and even feel the things that you feel. Our actions, emotional states and decisions are all based upon what we feel, think and perceive. Many times our actions, emotional states and decisions are affected by the pain of our past.

If a person who has been molested grows up to choose a life of promiscuity, that choice most likely has nothing to do with authenticity. Rather, it is a decision that has been birthed from pain. Transformation will occur when the journeyer is able to see in exactly what ways the darkness has affected them. When this is realized, the caterpillar will begin to turn into a beautiful butterfly!

Empowerment

Many times when we tell the story of transformation, we assume that the story ends when the caterpillar changes from its old form into a butterfly. We feel the story has ended because we are able to witness the beauty of this creature, knowing what it was when the process began.

But that is just the beginning of the story. The life of the butterfly is just beginning! It's important to understand that, after you have been transformed, your journey does not end. When the butterfly leaves its cocoon, it has a world to venture out in and experience. After the butterfly leaves its cocoon, it's important that it understands the world it now lives in. The better the butterfly understands its new world, the more it will be able to experience it to the fullest!

The third step of the journey is empowerment. When you decide to make a conscious change from a world of darkness to one of the light, you will notice many things to learn. When you have been transformed, you will exist on a higher level of consciousness. It's important that you understand this is order to be effective in your walk.

This new existence revolves around energy and your ability to harness and manipulate it for the positive advancement of humankind. You will become empowered when you understand how the world has been fashioned and constructed. When you understand how it works and how you can influence it, you will have the ability to help people that you once thought it impossible to help. You will have knowledge about this world that you have only read about in the bible and other great books. The true abilities of humanity will be understood in this stage of the journey.

Expansion

The final step of the journey is known as expansion. Within all creatures, there is a drive to procreate. Every living creature lives its life with the desire to reproduce. This instinctive drive is necessary for the continuation of all living things. Likewise on your journey, the need to reproduce is necessary; however, the process occurs differently than in nature.

Spiritual reproduction revolves around our desire, as the carriers of the light, to share the light we have with others. This part of the process is just as important, if not more so, than us bearing the light as individuals. The process of spiritual reproduction is so important because as those who carry the light increase, darkness will decrease. The only way the world and the overall consciousness of humanity will change for the better is if darkness is eradicated. Once darkness is eradicated, the kingdom of God will manifest in its fullness here on planet earth!

Religious institutions have been looked to as the main conduit for this process to happen. People gather together every Friday, Saturday, or Sunday to go to various worship centers, churches, synagogues, temples or mosques to receive spiritual insight. This is a necessary part of the advancement of people; however, the process cannot be limited to a place.

The light cannot and should not be reserved for a particular place. It must be shared by and with all people of the world. As you learn to walk in the light, you will also learn how to share it. Expansion is that process. The light grows by way of your willingness to accomplish this task.

It is my desire that you prepare yourself for this wonderful journey. The journey changed my life and I am certain it will do the same for you. I want you to know, you will not be alone in this process.

At the beginning of each chapter, you will notice a diary entry of sorts. These entries come from the diary of a creature named Luxor. After each phase of his journey, he wrote about his experiences. Within the very last chapter of the book, you will learn Luxor's story. Like you and I, he started off in the darkness; each entry is an account of what he experienced at each stage of his journey. I am certain you will often find that his feelings mirror yours at each stage of your journey.

You will also notice Challenges at the end of each chapter. The challenges are designed to move you towards the implementation of some good habits that helped me. The challenges are important to your growth because they will help you to really participate in exercises that will move you towards the level of understanding you need for the change that you want.

Your life is about to change, and at the end of this process, you will be a new creature. If you are looking to remain in the place that you are in right now, of confusion, depression, anxiety and lack of guidance, then this book isn't for you. However, if you desire to read something that will not only show you where the problem is, but lead you to a permanent solution, then my friend, you are in the right place! The state that you reside in now is not your home. You are not a product of what you see. You come from a place that is full of Joy, love, happiness and peace. You are not of this world and when you have completed this journey, you will fully understand how beautiful your home really is!

-JLW

Chapter 1

The World of Darkness

In the darkness, I cannot see my way—in the darkness, I do not know what my next step should be. Give me light in order that my fears may leave. For I know wherever there is light, darkness cannot exist...

You are sitting in a room that is absent of light, sound and comfort. Nothing is certain except for the fact that your consciousness is full of fear, doubt and uncertainty. You're in a relationship, but feel lonelier than ever. You've got a good job, but dread sitting down at your desk every day. You had dreams once, but aren't sure what happened to them. This is the feeling that leads most to the understanding that there is indeed a problem. Your world is dark, absent of any form of certainty and it is in desperate need of the light.

The World of Darkness is a troubling place for any soul to reside. After living in the dark world for an extended period of time, our eyes adjust to the absence of light. We do all that we can to move around that place, even though we are unable to see what our next step should be.

This becomes a problem for us, because all of our actions are based upon what we think instead of what we know. When I am able to see, my steps are calculated and precise; however, when I am walking in the World of Darkness, my successes and failures occur by chance or stroke of luck. If my happiness or failures depend upon chance, I don't know how to preserve a state of happiness or leave a state of unhappiness.

What is the World of Darkness?

I remember the day I fell into the World of Darkness. May 3rd, 2011 was a tough day for me. Around 4:30 p.m., the weight of the world came crashing down upon my shoulders. I immediately felt stressed, heavy, burdened down, weary, full of doubt. What happened? That's the million-dollar question—I don't know! I wasn't watching, listening to, or conversing with any person that would compromise my spirit.

These feelings are atypical for me. I am normally happy, energetic, joyful, positive, and focused; however, a dark cloud was over me and I couldn't shake it. I had feelings of doubt, lustful thoughts; I craved foods that were unhealthy and bad for my temple. I had streaks of anger and even dreams that were far from positive. What was happening to me? Was I losing it? Was I going crazy? Had some sort of spirit unknowingly attached itself to me, trying its best to capture the light that had been given to me by Christ?

When I got to the dark place, I was able to recognize that it was not my home. I had to do something, but I didn't know what to do. I wanted to quit, I had no inspiration, I felt as if my life stood for nothing. As I read the Word of God I saw nothing but black letters on thin, white, transparent pieces of paper—at that moment, even the Word of God seemed impotent to me.

The World of Darkness is not a place, but rather a state of being. We dwell in this common place whenever we find ourselves in constant states of confusion, disillusionment, frustration, anger, depression, anxiety as well as other like emotional and spiritual states. You may find yourself in this place as a frequent visitor, but sometimes we take up permanent residency.

If you find yourself constantly having arguments or feeling like the world is "getting on your nerves," if you have feelings of jealousy and envy towards others, if you frequently feel *blah,* if you're worried and nervous about what life holds—you're residing in the World of Darkness.

No good things come as a result of living in this place. Life lacks meaning, happiness is nonexistent, joy only appears in your dreams—this is a place that no soul made by God is designed to experience or endure. When humankind is isolated from the light of the sun, the body is deprived of essential vitamins and minerals. In a relatively short time, bones become brittle and psychosis will even creep its way into the mind. The absence of light is detrimental to the human body. Likewise, we must understand the soul was not designed to be out of communion with the pure, unrefined light from which it came.

Without sunlight, the body essentially begins to decompose. Likewise, when the soul is not exposed to the light of happiness, joy, peace, and love, it begins to long for its home. This causes its keeper, the body that the soul resides in, to continually exist in a state of misery. The state of misery that is often experienced while being in the World of Darkness is the soul's defense mechanism, allowing the person to understand that they must leave this place or face consequences that could be potentially life-threatening.

Are you living in this place? Do you find yourself in a constant state of misery, pain and discontentment? Do you have strong urges to leave but do not know where to go? Are you experiencing joy, love and peace in brief spurts, but the good feelings flee as quickly as they come? You were not designed to remain in this state. It is not your home.

You want to change, but you don't know how. Your life becomes hell on earth because you are unable to tap into the joys of your existence. When we dwell in this unnatural place, we do all that we can to cope, but most do not attempt to leave this place because they believe that's just how it is. We have been trained to deal with our problems ourselves, so we turn to our own understanding.

The World of Darkness breeds spirits of the dark world. These spirits are evil, satanic and wish to do all that they can to suck the goodness from the vessels of those who reside there. Those who live in the dark world are not all themselves evil; however, when we are forced to remain in a place that we were not made to survive in, we become a part of the place that brings us so much pain.

As we live in the world of confusion, anger and fear, these feelings can bleed us of our light. When we are bled of the light that is happiness, peace and joy, we often look for it in other ways. Many times, we stumble out of the sheer desire to feel good. It's in the dark world where spirits of addiction often attacks us. These spirits can attack us with many faces.

Lustful Sex

The human brain has a natural pleasure center, which allows for the production of endorphins. Endorphins are "neurotransmitters manufactured by the brain to reduce pain and induce a feeling of euphoria." [1]

The World of Darkness stifles our ability to naturally produce these feelings of euphoria. We are vessels of light, made to be filled with light, which is a byproduct of happiness, joy and peace. When we are unable to be what we were made to be, we long to have those feelings even if they are caused by unnatural pleasures of the dark world.

The process of engaging in sexual relations to the point of orgasm releases an abundance of endorphins. This process is pleasurable for human beings; however, the experience is one that does not last. "The endorphins released during orgasm create a temporary, but intense, sense of well-being." [2]

These brief but intense feelings can become a conduit to addiction for a person who dwells in the dark world. Though they are deprived of light while living in the dark world, the desire to "feel good" forever stays with that person.

---

[1] Judy Ford and Rachel Greene Baldino, *The Complete Idiot's Guide to: Enhancing   Sexual Desire* (New York: Penguin Group, 2007), 243.

[2] Cindy M. Meston, Ph.D. and David M. Buss, PhD, *Why Women Have Sex: Understanding Sexual Motivations--From Adventure to Revenge (And Everything In Between)* (New York: Times Books, 2009) 251.

Many times, an individual will act on feelings of depression in order that the pain may temporarily subside. If this individual is ignorant to his true state and the causes of his problems, he will remain in that realm, doing all that he can to prolong the good feelings. Once orgasm is achieved, the person finds a temporary state of pleasure; however, the feelings of ecstasy soon subside and he returns to his original state of misery.

This process becomes a recurring cycle—achieving temporary states of bliss punctuated by periods of sadness or other negative emotions. As the cycle continues, that state of satisfaction becomes ever more difficult to reach. The wanderer in the dark world jumps from one soul to the next, stealing the light that it has lost from others. The person is never satisfied, but becomes more and more of a sexual deviant, doing things that cross the line of sexual normalcy and intimacy.

Has sex become your opiate? Has this spiritual union and expression of authentic love been something you have abused for the temporary state of ecstasy that it brings you? As you indulge with multiple partners and endless sessions of masturbation, do you find yourself lonely, lost and overwhelmingly disappointed with where you are? This is the case because when we walk and wander in the dark world, we are ignorant to the direction of the light. The light is what you really want; however, you settle for the endless rings of self-torture that bring you to your current state.

Drug and Alcohol Abuse

Like sex, alcohol and drugs both have a direct correlation to the release of endorphins. These illicit substances cause those who consume them to feel overwhelming feelings of ecstasy and bliss. Whereas an orgasm lasts for a few seconds, the effects of drugs and alcohol can last for several hours. In essence, the person remains in a state of bliss for as long as the drug affects their senses.

Just as with those who develop addictions to sex, dependency and tolerance levels to the substances increase. As the person continues to pursue those feelings of ecstasy, they require greater amounts of the drug to produce the same level of pleasure that they experienced as a new user.

The manacles of the dark world can be overwhelming for all who experience its grasp. Those who do not understand spirituality or what has happened and what is happening to them often resort to these harmful outlets to create a temporary separation from their lonely world.

When you look at the effects of sex, drugs, and alcohol on human beings you find a consistency: All of them directly manipulate the body's pleasure centers. Wounded souls often reach out to these Band-Aids for temporary relief, without understanding the effects or the spiritual consequences of their actions. Drinking too much can cause job loss and health issues like cirrhosis of the liver. Sexual promiscuity can lead to low self-esteem, unwanted pregnancy and disease. Abuse of illegal or prescription drugs can cause financial and legal strain or death.

The truth of the matter is, when a person gets involved in these activities or ingests these chemicals, they are searching for happiness. Feeling good or happy is not a byproduct of the physical world; rather, it is a spiritual and emotional state of existence. This, then, becomes a trap for those caught up in the World of Darkness. They reach for physical measures of fulfillment in order to satisfy spiritual deficiencies.

This action creates a continual wheel, which never allows the person to achieve authentic happiness. When a person is authentically happy, their joy is not connected to anything of this world. It's not based on them having a lot of money or living in a certain home.

When a soul continues to reside in the dark world for any amount of time, the by-product of that state will sap the individual of all happiness, joy and peace. Happiness, joy and peace release the same endorphins as sex, drugs and alcohol. When a person is in the light and not in the darkness, they are able to control these natural feelings of happiness without the repercussions of addiction or chemical dependency.

If people who reside in the dark world are shown how to live in the light, their desire to look for external ways to feel good will forever leave them. They will never reach for anything or any person to lift them from their state, because they understand that the light comes from within.

Extended Stay in the Dark World

No Sense of Purpose

There are many people who recognize that they are inhabitants of the dark world. We might find ourselves in continual states of loneliness, depression, or anger. Once we understand how it has impacted our lives and our ability to enjoy the life we live, we want to free ourselves from this place. However, we're unsure as to how to make that happen.

When souls remain in the World of Darkness, all inhabitants experience certain repercussions. For one, a sense of purpose will be lost. Every soul that exists possesses consciousness or awareness of a purpose. Within the world in which we reside, purpose is often reduced to an action or a position. For example, many of us equate becoming a minister, doctor, lawyer, saving a person's life, or helping to create some law that feeds the hungry with having a purpose. When purpose is misunderstood as an action or as a position, it causes our focus to be outward and not inward.

Authentic purpose has nothing to do with doing; instead, it has everything to do with being. Authentic purpose is a state of consciousness whereby the soul, mind and body are in perfect harmony and unity. We are human beings, not human doings.

Many people who are living in the World of Darkness have issues discovering their purpose. Feelings of frustration and unhappiness are regular occurrences. These individuals will do all that they can to discover their purpose in life. They will read books, go to seminars and spend countless time and energy focused on this discovery.

A person who dwells in the World of Darkness is unable to find her true self for two reasons.

1.) She is looking in the wrong direction. She may say, "If only I had a new job or a new relationship," thinking that new friends and opportunities will cause the negative feelings that she experiences to dissipate; however, this is far from the case. Even when new relationships, jobs, and territories are explored, the same empty feelings and lack of true fulfillment will exist because the problem is not in an outward direction. The issue is from within. It is not a question of doing, but being.

2.) The second reason purpose is never found in this state is because the World of Darkness causes each inhabitant's mind, body and soul to be out of sync. What allows us to function in the realm of the supernatural, to know what we do not see, to see what we cannot touch, and accomplish what seems to be impossible is one's ability to maintain an interconnected state of mind, body and soul. When my mind and soul are connected, I am able to have revelations that do not require the process or the time needed for logic.

When the soul is out of sync, the person becomes dependent upon the mind. All things are understood through the conduit of logic, which within its own existence is flawed. With logic, the present and the past are the only two dimensions of time on which it can offer any insight. Logic's only context is what is happening and what has already happened.

When the soul is in constant communion with the mind, it operates on a higher plane than simple logic. It doesn't need to analyze the present or past to be accurate. It gives insight and direction that transcend time and logic. The union can never exist within the World of Darkness. Only those who walk in the light can experience the soul connected in harmony with the mind.

Jesus told Nicodemus, "I tell you the truth, no one can see the kingdom of God unless he is born again." [3] The authentic process of "rebirth" is the deliverance from the World of Darkness. When a person is reborn, thoughts, actions and experiences are all different. In this transformation, the world of the light, as well as the manifestations of that world, become experience. Before, it simply was not possible.

No Sense of Direction

The dark world not only strips its inhabitants of a sense of purpose, but also convolutes any sense of direction. Lack of direction and no sense of purpose are often experienced in tandem. Where there is one, there will certainly be the other. The "next step" in life cannot be something that is discovered or understood by logic. Know the "next step" is a byproduct of the soul and not the mind.

The soul and the mind can at times disagree, because the mind is only able to understand the present and the past. The disagreement between the soul and the mind occurs because the mind is unable to possess any understanding as it relates to the future.

------

[3] John 3:3 NIV Translation

The mind can only "predict" what the future holds. Predictions are always derived from the calculations and occurrences of the past. Predictions are consistent with statistical possibilities. The higher the instance of similar events that have occurred in the past, the more accurate a prediction can be. Statistics and possibilities are consistent of margins. The margins contain the possibility of error. When the mind attempts to understand the future, it is based on a certain occurrence with the possibility of that prediction being erroneous.

This method becomes a person's only way to navigate through the dark world. The soul is unable to communicate with the mind, so the person is totally dependent upon the mind, logic and its erroneous sense of understanding to order their steps. Relationships, friendships, opportunities and the like are all investigated and decided from the vantage point of logic and understanding that the mind presents. People oftentimes find themselves in situations that they never would have chosen, but they were unable to see it coming because it had not happened to them before and they could not predict the events that led up to it.

I have been in the dark world, and for this reason I know what it feels like and what it looks like. When I lived in that place, I had no sense of direction. My only measure of if I was in the right place revolved around humanistic interpretations of success, such as the reception of money, acclaim or reward for something I had done. When the mind is used to navigate through life, man-made interpretations of success are the only systems of measurement available; however, they do not always prove that we have done the right thing or made the best decision.

I became addicted to man's approval of my actions and thoughts. If I was not rewarded or appreciated by others, I felt as if what I had done was incorrect. This can be the farthest thing from the truth. When a person is delivered from the dark world, the person is able to see that things that are not acknowledged or appreciated by others are sometimes exactly what needs to be done. When a person is delivered from the dark world, direction comes from the soul and not the mind.

The soul does not need calculations or possibilities. These things are only needed when there is the possibility of error. The soul gives direction because it knows, not because it thinks. The soul leads and guides us places that are optimal for our spiritual growth, not for our sense of belonging amongst people. If logic could see what the soul understands, it would never guide you in that direction, because the mind abides by the first law of nature, self-preservation.

How many times have you ever been in situations that were uncomfortable to go through; however, you became a better person as a result of that experience? How many times have you found yourself in relationships that caused you physical pain, but spiritual satisfaction?

The Mind's True Role

Human beings are more than the physical vessel called the human body. Human beings have souls, which are merged with the mind and the body. The only purpose of the mind is so that we as spiritual beings are able to experience a physical reality—the mind allows that to occur. Each person is made to be governed by the soul, not the mind.

As stated earlier, when dwelling in the World of Darkness, the effects of that state remove all forms of light. When there is no light, there is no communion between the soul and the mind; the person becomes a slave to their mind instead of allowing the mind to be a worker of the soul. When this occurs, the soul becomes detached from the consciousness of the person. It is present; however, the person is neither aware of it nor the true nature of his reality.

At this point, the only experiences that are real to the person are those things that can be understood by the mind. The mind is so limited in its ability to process total consciousness that it causes the reality of the person to be flat and one-dimensional. Relations are topical, experiences are driven by humanistic reward (money, fame, credentials), life becomes worshipped and death is looked upon as the final end of all things.

This person does not truly understand his authentic nature, and therefore limits his ability to connect with all things through his soul. The human body is not a thing, "it is a process. At any instant in that process the constituent components of spirit, mind and body that comprise a human being bear a particular relationship to one another, a specific degree of interpretation each with the others. Our awareness of this interpretation constitutes the 'event' we perceive as ourselves."⁴ When there is no interpretation of the soul for the observer, things within the realm of the spirit cannot be understood or clearly interpreted.

This concept fuels the foundation of the atheist. Atheists reject God or anything above and beyond the physical reality. When all things of the soul are rejected, nothing outside of the mind's understanding is accepted as truth. For this reason, many scientists, physicists, mathematicians and doctors are atheists. Academia and atheism oftentimes go hand-in-hand because within science, math and other "exact studies," human logic and research is praised as the ultimate empirical system of understanding. Anything that is outside of that system is rejected because it cannot be logically proven.

The mind was not designed to be or to know all things. It was only designed to help each soul on the journey of this physical reality. When a person lives in the dark world, they are often unable to escape it because they are unable to understand and know that there is a better life beyond the one that is seen. You cannot lead a person out of the dark world, because without the light he is unable to see that the world that he resides in is dark. Instead, you must show him the slightest form of light and point him in its direction, in order that he may find it for himself.

---

⁴ John Burns *Foundations of a Global Spiritual Awakening* (Bloomington: Self Published John Burns) 2003, 3.

Checking Out of the World of Darkness

The dark world is no place for any soul to reside. The dark world is full of anger, hate, lust, envy, depression, revenge and the like. If you are in the dark world, you must do all that you can to walk in the direction of the light. How can this be done? If you want to see the light, you must understand how the darkness has affected your present life.

This can be tricky, because when you are in the dark world you may feel as though you do see the light—but you don't. The light you are witnessing is artificial. It's not authentic. You must see for yourself how anger, lust, fear and depression have prevented you from communing with your soul and blocked you from the source that recharges your being. When you are able to make the connection between the two, you will desire to leave from where you are.

At the moment of this realization, the instinctive nature of the soul will take over like a mother caring for her young. She knows what to do and where to go. The soul functions in the same way. When you are able to see how the dark world has kept you from freedom, you will begin to seek new relationships, wisdom, friends and associates as well as thoughts. It is at this point that your walk begins. If you desire to take the first step of that journey, adhere to this challenge.

Challenge

Part 1: What negative emotional or spiritual state do you find yourself experiencing the most? Is it anger, impatience, lust, selfishness, greed etc.? Really take time to identify what this is, because it is key to your freedom. Once you have identified it, write it down in a book, journal or perhaps an electronic entry. When you begin to think about the question, you may have more than one emotion that comes to the forefront of your consciousness. If this is the case, write that down as well.

Part 2: Once you have made note of these various emotional states, take each state and write them down on a different piece of paper. Write the state at the top of the page ("Anger"), and underneath the title, write down every major occurrence you can remember whereby that emotional or spiritual state has caused negativity in your life. Do this with each emotion that is on your list. Take as much time needed, ensuring the fact that you compose each memory that you have and how that emotional or spiritual state has affected you.

What to Expect

If done correctly, you will begin to remember things, people, experiences and places that you thought you had forgotten. Pain, tears, fear and many times anger will be birthed from this exercise. You will begin to see how your time in the dark world has shaped your personality. You will see how it has impacted relationships with family members and friends. You will begin to view yourself and the world differently. You will see many opportunities that you missed as a result of the dark world. You will understand why you are the way that you are.

If this occurs, you know you have spent ample time with this challenge. If you do not experience this, it is an indication that you have not spent enough time thinking about how the emotional and spiritual states have negatively impacted you.

When you experience the revelations of this challenge, you will still be in the dark world; however, you will then understand that it is not your home. Before reading the next chapter, be certain to spend time with this chapter until you received that revelation. When you receive it, you will be ready for the next step.

Chapter 2

Walking in the Light

Before this moment, darkness covered me. My sight was absent, my path was never made clear. I have been freed from the darkness; however, the light now shows me the magnitude of my state. I'm torn, tattered and scarred, yet I am still here to see a New Day. I will pull myself up from this place of pain and follow the light, which will lead me to a place of permanent joy and peace. I anticipate what is to come, now that I know my steps will lead me to my eternal divine destiny.

"In the beginning, God created the heavens and the earth. And the earth was without form, and void; and darkness was upon the face of the deep. And the spirit of God moved upon the face of the waters. And God said, 'Let there be light,' and there was light."[1]

There are two belief systems that dominate modern thought as it pertains to creation. The first thought revolves around the "Intelligent Design" theory. Intelligent Design (ID) assumes as fact that "there is a fundamental evidence that a mind lies behind the origin of life and the universe."[2] ID would be supported by most religions, which believe that God or some Supreme Being(s) intelligently designed the world, galaxies and the universe.

The "Big Bang Theory" is the commonly accepted counterpart to ID. The "Big Bang Theory" states that

---

[1] Genesis 1:1-3 KJV

[2] H. Wayne House, *Intelligent Design 101* (Grand Rapids: Kregel Publications) 2008, 28.

the origins of time, space and this present physical reality began with a sudden explosion or massive presence of energy which set all things into motion, leading to the creation of planets as well as the evolution of humankind. [3]

Those who believe in God accept that God "created the heavens and the earth." Those who believe in evolution accept the premise that all things were created by an explosion.

Even though these are two competing schools of thought, both maintain that energy was the impetuous force leading to the creation of all things. In Genesis Chapter 3, the force was called, "light." That force was the entity that started the movement of all things. Without it there was nothing: the world was empty, dark and without purpose. When light is introduced to darkness, it lends itself to change in all things.

Light is the authentic origin of all things in the physical and spiritual realm. Light exists authentically whenever something is existing in the way it was created to exist. The light is pure, absolute and limitless. A person who walks in the light is a person who lives out a reality that is in line with his divine purpose. This becomes problematic, because every human being alive sometimes confuses their real and true nature.

The authentic nature of humankind is not a body, but rather a soul. The only way for a person to walk in the light at all times is if that person experiences a

---

[3] Tom Van Flandern, *Dark Matter Missing Planets and New Comets* (Berkeley: North Atlantic Books) 1993, 95.

change or a rebirth and refocuses his center. The center of that person must not revolve around ego, but rather around their true nature—their soul.

The dark world prevents all of its inhabitants from realizing the true nature of reality. People in the dark world live to satisfy the flesh. The more the flesh is fulfilled and fed, the more people become detached from their authentic selves.

Finding Your Way to the Light

In the first chapter, you learned that the dark world was not a physical place but an emotional state. It's a place of anger, lust, fear, loneliness and confusion. The dark world is the place whereby you are completely detached from the essence of your soul. Every person desires to be happy, to have peace and to continually dwell in a place of joy and inner contentment. All persons want this; however, it can never be permanently achieved until a person walks in the light.

Just as the world of darkness is an emotional state, so is walking in the light. Walking in the light occurs when I am able to live my life with intentions and ordered steps. This occurs when I reconnect with my spirit and soul and I detach myself from the need to satisfy my body or my flesh. The process of moving from the dark world to walking in the light is an act of being "re-centered." When you become re-centered, you become a person who experiences a different reality. When you become re-centered, the following experiences take on a whole new light.

Relationships

In the dark world, relationships revolve around the comfort of self. While living in the dark world, I always selected friends who made me feel good. I selected people who supported me in all the things that I did. All along, I never understood that these individuals around me were not helping me. Rather, they were hindering me. Just because a person makes you feel good at all times does not mean that this person helps you to grow or to become the person that you need to be.

My friends allowed me the opportunity to do things that were not of God, and I appreciated them because they didn't judge me. My friends never challenged my words or thoughts, because they felt that by agreeing with me, they were being good to and for me.

When I became re-centered, when I began to walk in the light, I noticed I had a different outlook on relationships. I moved from desiring friends to desiring spiritual partners. Every person in your life should assist you in your spiritual growth. If your "friends" are not helping you to become a better person, they are people who keep you in that place of darkness. Ask yourself these questions:

1.) Are the friends in my life actively making positive contributions towards me becoming a better person?

2.) Have I taken the time to share with my friends my spiritual goals and desires?

3.) Are the people in my life able to propel me towards the place that I need and desire to be?

When I began to walk in the light, I started to view those around me not as buddies or friends, but as partners who invest in me as I invest in them. Life is a journey, and all who enter your life should help you on that journey as you help them. No person who ever entered your life or you theirs was there by accident. All relationships have purpose; however, when you walk in the light, you are able to more clearly see what that purpose is.

When I resided in the world of darkness, I oftentimes confused the nature of my relationships with the people in my life. For example, I used to think whenever I was attracted to a person that it meant I should pursue them in a romantic way. But sometimes the people in our lives with whom we pursue romantic relationships are not designed to be lovers, but rather, spiritual partners.

There are times when you meet a person and you experience a strong attraction to them. You think of them and you even dream of them. When residing in the dark world, those authentic feelings are often misinterpreted. The true attraction is not to their physical body, but to their soul. That person was in your life, not for the purpose of dating, but rather for the purpose of mutual spiritual development.

Spiritual union isn't about gender or sex, and it has nothing to do with romance. Spiritual partnership differs from a friendship or romantic relationship, because that person is in your life to help you grow in various elements of your spiritual journey. Instead of building a relationship based on fun or meeting physical needs, the focus is on growth and evolution.

If you and I are spiritual partners and I know you have a drinking problem, I will counsel you to work on your issue. I'm not concerned that you might be offended or dislike my advice. A platonic friend might know your drinking is a sore subject and avoid discussing it in order to prevent friction.

How many times have you found yourself destroying a union of spiritual partnership in your life because you pursued a physical relationship? This happens when we are not walking in the light. When you walk in the light, you can see things and people for what they are. Your senses become honed and precise. You are given more insight into situations. You become more deliberate in your resolve not to allow the flesh to interfere with the union of two souls.

Wisdom

What exactly is wisdom? Wisdom is knowledge and understanding that is not gained from the confines of the mind. Wisdom is knowing without having to investigate. Feeling the presence of something without seeing it. Wisdom is arriving at a place or point of understanding without the process of logic as the conduit. Wisdom can only occur when the observer is living and existing with the spirit of the soul and not the ego.

Inhabitants of the dark world can only experience that realm by way of the mind. While operating with the mind as the primary point of understanding, the observer is unable to tap into the knowledge and wisdom that only the soul possesses.

The ego is the enemy of all humankind. "Egoism is the most dangerous weakness of Man. It leads to the downfall of the spiritual aspirant. On account of egoism, one considers himself the doer. Egoism blocks the flow of the Divine Energy."[4]

Divine energy is the light. It is the source that causes us to be exactly who and what we were made to be. Understanding is found within the soul, not within the mind. When I existed within the dark world, I made all decisions based on logic, which is the method of reasoning that the mind uses to function. I found myself always making bad decisions that I eventually regretted. Allow me to ask you a few questions to see if you are absent of the light. Allow this to be a guide that helps you to move in the right direction.

Do you find yourself desiring or wanting to know what the next major step is in your life? Do you find yourself at a standstill, not knowing what to do or where to go? This is indicative of living in the dark world. So many people attempt to find direction through logical sense. People who find themselves in this stalled state have allowed something to block the light or divine energy that keeps us in contact with our soul.

When you walk in the light, you find yourself in complete communion with divine energy. Some people consider this the voice of God or the presence of God. In this state, you don't wonder or ask yourself the question, "What do I do now?" There is no need to ask yourself this question, because you know what the next step is.

---

[4] Dr. Aparna Chattopadhyay, Perals of Spiritual Wisdom (Khari Biaoli, Delhi Pustak Mahal) 2003, 32.

You live life with certainty and a sense of confidence, knowing your current actions are in line with your destiny. No longer do you judge your steps based upon the money you may gain or the acclaim you may receive from other people. These things are no longer of importance to you, therefore your decisions will be more authentic. Authenticity is pure communion with divine energy.

Do you finding yourself holding on to traumatic experiences of your past? Are there things that you find yourself continually reliving because of the magnitude of the event? Have you been shaped by the pain of divorce, rape, incest, infidelity, domestic violence, or the death of a loved one? People who are unable to move past life experiences are people who are unable to walk in the light.

The circumstance of those who reside in the dark world as well as those who walk in the light can often times be the same; however, the way they experience these circumstances are very different. When I was residing in the realm of darkness, I had the mentality of a victim. I would say things like, "Why is this happening to me?" or "Why am I going through this?" The statement and the mental state revolve around the ego. As we learned earlier, the ego stops the flow of light or divine energy. Now that I am walking in the light, I still experience some of the same unfortunate circumstances; however, my reactions are different because walking in the light changes the observer's perspective.

When I am walking in the light, I have a different view. I do not analyze my experiences through the lens of the mind or logic. I see all of the negative things that I've experienced as stepping stones which allow me to access the next level of my life.

No longer must we hold the death of a loved one against anyone, asking, "Why did my child have to leave me so soon?" This question is not asked by those who walk in the light, because the question is one that is formulated to appease the logic of the mind. Questions such as, "Why was I cheated on?" are not asked because the soul does not need logical explanations. When you walk in the light, you will become authentically empowered by every experience.

Joy and Happiness

When you decide to walk in the light, joy and happiness will not be temporary conditions created by external things, but a place wherein you reside at all times. If you temporarily lose your way, you will have an understanding as to how to return to it.

The place of joy and happiness becomes permanent because it is not attached to circumstances. The dark world is such a depressing place because happiness and joy are always attached to circumstances, such as money, love, sex, position, power, fame etc. These are inauthentic things that are fabrications of a false reality. The soul is unable to interpret their significance; therefore, it does not respond to them.

The soul responds when it is balanced, centered and connected to its origin—the light. When it is exposed to the light, it is nourished and satisfied because it resides in a place of familiarity.

How happy would your life be, if your state of joy and happiness had nothing to do with anything around or outside of you? How would your life change if the people you trusted never robbed you of happiness, or if the economy never caused you to worry? How would you feel if relationships that ended never pushed you to the point of emotional turmoil?

This seems far-fetched, but it can be attained. You must learn how to walk in the light. Once you have mastered the journey, you will learn that you are the creator of all the things that you experience. Your happiness, joy, pain and sorrow are all birthed from within you. As your perspective changes, so will your experiences. ? Real joy comes from God

How Do I Walk in the Light?

The most logical question at this point of your journey should be, "So, how do I walk in the light?" Now you know and understand the dark world, as well as what it is to walk in the light. If you desire to know exactly what needs to be done in order to walk in the light, be certain to pay close attention to the following principles, because your ability to understand and apply them will determine your ability to achieve your spiritual goals.

Walking in the light requires each person to intentionally become aware of and change personal thoughts, words and actions. When these three areas of existence are addressed and adjusted accordingly, you will be in complete control of your experiences.

Thoughts

The most fundamental of all three areas is thought. The thoughts of every person are the foundation of what the person says as well as what the person does.

A person who is unaware of or out of control in their personal thoughts is a person who is out of control and unaware of where they are, as well as where they are going.

"Man is Made or unmade by himself; in the armory of thought he forges the weapons by which he destroys himself; he also fashions the tools with which he builds for himself heavenly mansions of joy and strength and peace." [5]

Most people who've just had a good day don't see that their experience started with how or what they were thinking. Likewise, most people who've had a bad day are unable to see that what they experienced was connected to their thoughts. All states of being, be it happiness, joy, peace, depression, anger, or hate are directly connected to the thoughts of the person experiencing them. When someone understands this, that person is able to position themselves as the architect of their own experiences.

If you desire to walk in the light, you must do all that you can to monitor your thoughts at all times. Here are three exercises you can do, which will help you achieve this.

1.) Start off every day believing you are blessed. Envision yourself experiencing the best day of your life. Have thoughts of being productive and fruitful. Tell yourself and believe that when you arrive to the place you are going, you will do all that you can to bring light to wherever there is darkness. Make this a daily practice and do all that you can to position yourself in a mood of positive thinking.

---

[5] James Allen, *As a Man Thinketh* (Sante Fe, Sun Publishing Company) 1983, 9.

Play music that encourages positive thinking. Don't accept phones calls from people who may cause you to have negative thoughts. Realize within yourself that you are in control of your circumstances and do all that you can to make this day the greatest day of your life! Really believe in your thoughts and accept them to be true, and when you leave your home you will leave with a different outlook on circumstances and people, as well as yourself. If you maintain this state of thinking, you will see the difference it makes.

2.) Constantly remain in total awareness of every thought. The moment something happens whereby your thoughts are no longer positive or in sync with what you want to manifest, do all you can at that very moment to change that thought. For example, if you are presented with a person who has a questionable, negative or angry countenance about themselves and it seems as if it is directed toward you, be mindful and aware of your thoughts. The moment you find yourself internalizing what is said to you, use the power of thought to keep those negative energies from changing your mood.

Understand that whatever that person says to you has nothing to do with you, but is rather a projection of what they feel about themselves. Say to yourself, "I have nothing to do with this; therefore I will not accept or allow their words or actions to affect me." Remain positive and refuse to argue with or complain to them. Remember, you are walking in the light, and when you desire to do that there will be people who will do all that they can to interfere with your journey.

3.) Maintain consistency with your challenges. As you attempt to control your thoughts, understand it is something you must practice each and every day. Just like anything else, practice is key. The more you attempt to control your thoughts, the better you will be at controlling them. Whenever you have an opportunity to control your thoughts, be certain to try—it will make a big difference on your spiritual journey.

Speaking positive is of thru my kids a goal my the journey to my

Words

The words that we speak are carriers of life or death. Indeed, "The power of life and death is in the tongue." [6] Once you exercise control over what you speak, you will find that the words you speak are different as well. It is up to you to be certain that every word that comes from your lips is of the light and not of darkness. There are a few areas you need to pay close attention to as you incorporate these principles in your life.

1.) Never allow anything negative to manifest as words that exit your mouth. If you always walk in the light, taking control over your thoughts, you will find this to be an easy task; however, whenever you are tempted to say anything negative, abstain at all costs by either remaining silent or saying something that is uplifting and positive instead.

If you receive bad news about your health, never go around speaking on how sick you are. When you do that, you plant seeds within your own consciousness and mind. Whatever is in the mind will grow and manifest into a real reality. If you lose your job, don't walk around speaking on how sad you are about it or

---

[6] Proverbs 18:21

how much you dislike your ex-boss. Instead, remain positive and reflect on what you learned and how you grew from the experience. Focus your thoughts on doing all you can to go to a new and higher dimension in your life.

2.) Always speak life to others. Realize that your words are seeds that are planted in the minds of others, which will manifest into a reality as well. Whenever someone presents you with rumors, gossip or negativity about any person or anything, NEVER speak negativity about it. NEVER give negative commentary—always walk in the light. Either keep your silence or challenge others to do so. Don't worry about appearing self-righteous; look upon yourself as a barrier of light.

When people know you do not entertain negativity, they will not spread it in your presence. That alone means you have brought light to darkness. Some people will stop desiring to be around you because of your new walk, but that's ok. It's ok, because like attracts like. Others who walk in the light will see yours and they will be attracted to it. As the community of light barriers grows, the amount of darkness the world sees will slowly diminish. The ultimate destruction of darkness on earth is the manifestation of God's kingdom on earth.

Actions

Each principle builds upon the next. If you start with your thoughts, your words will follow suit. Likewise if your thoughts and words are as they should be, your actions will change as well. The biggest way to change your actions is through your thoughts. If there are things you desire to stop doing or to lose the taste for, you must make adjustments to your thoughts. This is the only way to change your actions. The following examples can help you understand how.

1.) A number of people have excessive desires for sexual intercourse. These individuals are very sexually expressive and involved. Many of them desire to be more spiritual and connected to God, and they know lust and promiscuity are blocking this from taking place. But it seems no matter what they do to stop, nothing seems to work.

The first mistake that these individuals make is attempting to stop their behavior patterns while their thoughts remain the same. It's like a person with a drug problem who tries to quit but still reminisces about the good times they had on drugs. This will only work for so long. The only way the drug addict can leave the drugs alone is if they desire something else, i.e. a clean life, more than the artificial high.

People who find themselves addicted to sex will never completely abolish the desire to have sex, because human beings are made to procreate. However, their unhealthy actions can change if their thoughts are adjusted. These are a few tips that will help people in this transition.

A.) Be aware of the music you listen to. When you listen to sexually charged, seductive music it will alter your thoughts, which will therefore cause you to desire to act upon your thoughts.
B.) Surround yourself with people who are respectful of your desire to change. You are only as strong as those who support you in your spiritual goals and desires.

C.) Allow your understanding of sex to change. Do not allow yourself to view sex as an event whereby the body is satisfied, but rather something that allows you to connect with a person spiritually.

D.) Understand the fact that every sexual partner shares your soul. In this light, casual sex should be viewed quite differently. These are basic steps that should help you align your thoughts in ways that propel you toward your goals and desired destination.

If we become cautious and intentional about our thoughts, words and actions, we will continue to walk in the light. When we walk in the light, we will witness a life that is full of joy, happiness and peace. Now that you understand the basic fundamentals of walking in the light, allow the challenge below to be a practical guide in your quest.

Challenge

For the next week, allow this challenge to be a spiritual fast of sorts. For the next seven days, you will do all that you can to walk in the light. Each day, make a commitment to do three different, intentional, and deliberate things.

1.) Commit yourself to monitoring your thoughts at all times. When you rise, focus your thoughts on having a great day. Expect to be successful and productive. Anticipate each day being the greatest day of your life!

2.) Commit yourself to monitoring your words. This week you will allow nothing negative to exit your mouth. You will not participate in gossip, negative statements about yourself or others, and you will not comment on anything unless the words are positive.

3.) Monitor you actions. See if you can make a connection with how your actions are connected to your thoughts. When you are able to clearly see this, you will be able to adjust your actions.

Once you finish the week, make notes of all the things you learned about yourself through the process. Do not read the next chapter until you have internalized and executed this challenge. The process of growth you will experience as a result of this challenge is the foundation for the next step!

My desire is to bless them with carnal things as a reward for their obedience and respect but I usually regret it because their negative behavior becomes dominate just as soon as they are satisfied

Things about myself:

Stress - it causes me to lose focus and then my situations compound in a way that I am overwhelmed. It is like as soon as one thing happens, yet another comes, then another, then another all within minutes of each other and I don't have a chance to catch my breath or refocus my thoughts.

When it comes to my kids, it seems as though they are determined to live a life of disobedience and disrespect. I work hard at teaching them God's ways and commandments. When they want something specific, they do things that they know are the right things to do (kiss up so to speak). But the second that they have received what they want, they have achieved their goal, they go back to their defiant, disobedient & disrespective ways. At those times I feel cheated, punked out. I regret whatever it was that I did for their joy.

Chapter 3

Discoveries of the Light

I now see the light. As I look around, I am able to see all that I once missed. My path is made clear; my friends and foes are distinguishable. My steps are ordered and my actions are full of intention. Without the light, I would not have been able to gain this wisdom I now possess. I have learned so much, yet there is so much more I need to receive.

Imagine the feeling of being blind your entire life; then one day, you suddenly receive your sight. How would that make you feel? You would be excited, happy and full of joy and thanksgiving. You would remain in a state of continual bliss and joy. You would look at the sky, examine the earth. You would spend days watching people and doing all of the things your inability to see had prevented you from doing and experiencing. Your life would change for so many reasons. You would be a new person because the darkness had robbed you of happiness, joy and direction, as well as imagination.

After spending some time exploring all that you had missed, you would then move to a place of reflection. After the initial excitement of seeing all of the great things exposed by the light, you would be in a state of personal discovery. You would reflect on how you had been lost, without direction. You would see the clutter and piles of stuff that were causing you to trip and fall as you tried to move around your house. You would notice all of the things that you had been unable to experience as a result of being blind.

At this moment, this is where you find yourself on your spiritual walk. You started off in the dark world, and now you have been exposed to the light. The initial feeling of walking in the light is such a wonderful experience. You live with direction, order, intention, joy, happiness and peace. You have learned how to control or alter your circumstances by proper thinking, positive words and purposeful actions. You have become a new creature, and you have made some new discoveries. You are now able to see how the world of darkness has negatively influenced your life.

The light exposed you to your current state, but more importantly it has shown you how all of the decisions of your past have negatively impacted your present and potential future. For so long, you were unable to see how your selection of thoughts, words and actions affected you, but now that you are in the light, you are able to see the results clearly.

Human beings have been created to exist in three different dimensions: the mind, body and soul. When you walk in the light, you make discoveries about each one. Once the light exposes to you the flaws acquired while living in total darkness, spiritual growth will begin.

When a child is born, he has a new life, parents, environment and opportunities. He has a clean state. However, this new life is foreign to him. The child must mature, grow and develop. As the child develops, his life will change. Since you have been walking in the light, you have become like that newborn baby. All of what you once knew is foreign to you now, and it is necessary for you to develop in a way that maximizes your abilities to become who and what you were made to be.

Mental Discoveries

Now that you are walking in the light, you are aware of the fact that your thoughts are the origin of all the things you are and have experienced. Now, you are able to see that all the times when you were depressed, lonely, afraid and full of fear, those feelings were directly connected to your thoughts. Unfortunately, you allowed yourself to make decisions while being in those various states. Now that you are walking in the light, you realize that if you desire to continue living in the light, you must address the manifestations of things done while living in the world.

Anger, fear, jealousy and other negative emotional states are repercussions of not walking in the light. We allow experiences to control our thoughts; therefore, our thoughts will lead to similar negative manifestations. When you are walking in the light, you become aware of your thoughts, as well as the feelings that transpire. As you do this over and over again, you are able to really see and understand the root of your anger, fear and jealousy. When you understand where something comes from, you understand how it has affected you and, therefore, how it can be eliminated.

If I am inside of my home and notice ants about, but never pay attention to the hole that is underneath the windowsill, it will be very difficult for me to rid my home of the ants. If, one day, I take the time to examine every crack and crevice in my house and then find this hole, I would then clearly see how the ants are entering my home.

Walking in the light allows us to see the holes in our personality. It allows us to better understand why we have the issues we have, which is a step in the direction of our healing. If I am a person who is often jealous of others, that jealousy will cause me issues so long as I remain that way.

The jealousy is similar to the ants in my home. Every time I see a person who has more than me, is doing something I have never done, or is purchasing something I cannot afford, I get envious. I find myself saying certain things about them to justify in my own consciousness why they have what they have, in order to make me feel better about myself. People like this often look down on others. The emotion of jealousy within them is just like the ants in the home: It's there, but they are completely ignorant as to how and why they came to be this way.

When a person who has issues of jealousy begins to walk in the light, the person becomes intentional about their thoughts. The person becomes fully aware of what they are thinking. When thoughts of jealousy arise and the person becomes aware of it, they are now able to understand where it is coming from.

At this moment, the lesson of the light is learned. The person who walks in the light now understands that the feelings of jealousy were never connected to the other person, but rather the insecurities within their own consciousness. At this moment, the hole has been identified! Now that it has been identified, the issues become clear.

As the person continues to walk in the light, the same process will happen with every single emotion: lust, anger, hate, fear, etc. The process follows the same analogy of the ants. When I find myself experiencing feelings of anger, the feeling is the presence of the ants in the home. However, when I am intentional about my thoughts, I am able to locate the hole, or true origin of the emotion. I am able to understand the true origin of my issue.

When this is done continually and effectively, the laws of attraction are put into play; however, the difference at this moment is the person begins to be in control of what is attracted. "The law of attraction creates a cocoon, so to speak, of like energy around each personality so that as it seeks to heal anger, or fear, or its jealousy, the metamorphosis process into wholeness is intensified and accelerated, is brought to the center of the stage of awareness."[1]

Walking in the light shifts a person's awareness. It allows the person to become aware of things they once ignored. Awareness is increased by three different means.

1.) The person becomes aware of what is being felt or experienced. If you walk around each day on rocks, stones and hard surfaces without wearing any shoes, the soles of your feet will develop additional skin so that you don't feel the sharp edges. If you proceed to have a pedicure, the dead skin that has developed on the soles of your feet will be removed, and you will begin to feel the stones and rocks on the ground. In essence, your awareness will change and be heightened. This is what happens to each person who decides to walk in the light. The awareness of how emotions impact your life will increase and become more prevalent to your consciousness.

---

[1] Gary Zukav, *The Seat of The Soul* (New York, Free Press) 2007, 210.

2.) The person becomes aware of how past emotions have shaped his present personality. Many people feel that how they act has everything to do with their personality and is just "how they are." This is dangerous because the person equates his or her ways with their personality. This is false. The one consistent personality trait held by all human beings is the trait of loving and desiring to be loved. Anything else that is added to this is a product of pain. People who are attitudinal, impatient, depressed or emotionally unstable have been shaped by negativity. These individuals have unknowingly attracted every negative experience into their life. When one decides to walk in the light, he is then able to see exactly how the negativity of his life has shaped him into the person that he is today.

[handwritten note in margin: Cop out to accepting change]

3.) When an individual is able to understand exactly what is wrong with him and how it has affected him, as well as the origin of the problem, the person is then equipped to know how to remove it. When we become physically ill, the doctor will order tests in order to examine the blood. Upon finding the results, the doctor is able to tell exactly what the problem is, where it is affecting the person and how to treat the condition. Walking in the light allows each person a window into their spiritual health. Instead of being ignorant to things that negatively and positively affect you, you are able to live life with more control and intention.

Physical Discoveries

As you make conscious decisions to live a more spiritual life, you will notice that you become a more "centered" person. The process of being "re-centered" occurs when the soul becomes the foundation of our awareness and not the mind. When this occurs, the person begins living to fulfill their authentic self, instead of living for those things that are inauthentic. When the soul is fulfilled through living in joy, happiness and peace, the person is able to live with purpose and freedom.

When we become re-centered, not only are we more in tune with our spiritual selves, we also notice a new connection with our bodies. All of my life, I've always gotten random blemishes on my face. Every time I looked in the mirror, it seemed to me that a new mark or blemish had appeared. This was very frustrating because I had no clue as to why I had the breakouts.

For years, I assumed it was just my skin type and hoped that it would be something that would change in time. But as I grew older, the blemishes continued and so did my frustration. What should I do? How could I change this issue that caused me so much discomfort and embarrassment?

At that moment, I begin to notice everything that I ate, drank or otherwise consumed. Certainly, there was some type of connection with what I had been eating. When I started to focus on my diet, I noticed that every time I ate onions, the blemishes would appear, when I did not eat them they would not! I had found my problem! For years, I had been plagued with this; however, when I took the time to focus on what I was consuming, I was able to discover my issue!

As we walk in the light, we must be in tune, not only with our thoughts, but also with the way our emotions affect us physically. The body is a wonderful indicator that will instantly notify you of any poisonous thoughts that need to be cleared from your consciousness. As you learn to connect yourself with these sensations, you will have another method of becoming free from the pain of poisonous thoughts.

Many times, you may find yourself experiencing physical pain. What you don't know is that the pain is directly connected to your present thoughts. For many of you, the pain you experience on a daily basis is connected to poisonous thoughts. Your thoughts are like the onions that caused blemishes on my face.

There are many people who experience headaches, tension, back pain, stomach ulcers, hypertension, a weakened immune system, weight gain, insomnia and even terminal illnesses like cancer as a direct result of poisonous thoughts. These individuals suffer from emotional toxicity, yet they are unable to know and understand the connection between their thoughts and physical ailments in the body. This is known as a "psychosomatic illness."

The word psychosomatic comes from two Greek words: psych (mind) and soma (body). [2] In essence, a psychosomatic illness is an illness found in the body which is connected to the mind. This goes to show that our mind, body and soul are all connected. Whether this is accepted or not, thoughts manifest in our body on a daily basis.

---

[2] Gordon Eldin and Eric Golanty, *Health and Wellness* (London, Jones and Barlett Publishers) 2010, 30.

Let's say you find yourself at the bank counter attempting to deposit a check after a long day of work. The day is nearing an end and you desperately desire to finish your errand in order to retire for the evening. While waiting your turn for the clerk to assist you, a person who has not waited for one minute enters the bank, rushes to the line and jumps ahead of you. At that moment, you find yourself becoming hot; your head pounds, sweat rolls down your brow, and you become totally consumed with rage.

We have all been in situations like that, when something happens that causes us to respond. This is a prime example of how an emotion (anger) quickly manifests and makes itself known in our body, by way of a pounding head and an increased temperature level. This is something all of us must understand, because when we understand it, we can prevent it.

The only way any thought can negatively manifest within the body of a person is if the person allows that thought to remain within their consciousness and responds to it. Back at the bank, when the man runs and cuts in line, the only way I will find myself with a throbbing head or getting hot all over is if I give the energy of anger to the fact that this man has broken line.

If I stay in the same position, but cause my thoughts to be positive, perhaps I could even look upon his breaking the line as a lifesaver. A lifesaver? Yes, I say a lifesaver, because what if there is an accident just up the street that would have been on my very path? Had I not been delayed by this person, I potentially could have been killed. Think on that for a minute. Would you rather a person cut ahead of you in line, or would you prefer to be next in line, yet lose your life 10 minutes later?

You are in control of your thoughts, and when you understand their effects on the body and the ways these thoughts can manifest, you will learn how to prevent them. What pains and issues are you dealing with physically that are directly connected to your poisonous thoughts? How many nights of sleep are you losing in a week's time because you are allowing high levels of emotional toxicity to drain your cells of their health, vigor and vitality? How much better would you feel if you knew exactly how your thoughts negatively impacted your body?

The only way to control these physical manifestations is by exploring the spiritual root of the problem. The following is an example of how to do that.

Many days, you find yourself with tense, tight shoulders. You roll your neck, seek the help of a massage therapist—you may even hire the services of a chiropractor. The only way to rid yourself of the pain is to seek professional help; however, as soon as you leave those individual sessions, the pain and tension returns. What's going on?

The shoulders, neck and upper back are associated with stress and overall feelings of anxiety. Over the course of the day, if you constantly worry about your job, family and personal life, that energy center becomes affected by those continual thoughts of anxiety.

Hypertension, heart problems and thyroid problems have all been directly associated with this energy center. Could the physical problems that you are encountering be attributed to your thoughts of worry and anxiety?

As you walk in the light, you will become more and more attuned to these sensations and feelings. You will notice how thoughts that you never paid any attention to before now cause you physical pain. Your increased sensitivity to the physical manifestations of poisonous thoughts will allow you the ability to change.

Emotions, both good and bad, are nothing more than forms of energy. In later chapters of this book, you will learn what energy is and how it works. Please allow this as an introduction to understanding how your thoughts impact your body.

Energy Centers and Negative Thoughts

There are seven energy centers within the body. These energy centers start at the crown of the head and run to the base of the spine. Each energy center is a mechanism by which energy flows through the body. The seven energy centers are constantly opening and closing, and the process of them opening or closing is what denotes their effect on the body.

When one of the energy centers opens too much, it is in direct correlation to a person dwelling on a certain problem. For example, when you find yourself stressed out and in a constant state of worry and fear, you are transferring energy to the center that controls your throat, neck and shoulders, increasing tension. It's a cycle: A person who is excessively caught up in a particular problem generally gives extra energy to the associated area. That area's energy center then becomes greatly opened, which pulls the person's attention even more to the area. [3]

---

[3] Genevieve Lewis Paulson, *Evolution In This Lifetime: A Practical Guide* (Saint Paul, MN: Llewellyn) 1991, 128.

As you continually worry about finances, relationships, your job or your work status, you cause excessive amounts of energy to affect the areas of your body associated with those specific emotions. This excessive energy causes issues within the body, especially the organs in those respective areas.

It makes sense, if you think of the things that cause you to relax and be stress-free. When you journey to the massage therapist, the therapist does all they can to make you relax and forget about your problems. You are resting in a comfortable room, listening to soothing music. The key to this being such an effective temporary fix is because the session tricks you into changing your thoughts and your focus.

When you leave the massage therapist, you feel so light and free. All of your troubles are gone and you feel refreshed. So what has occurred? During the process of your session, the energy center that was emitting too much power was closed and you became more balanced. As the energy center closes, the surrounding areas of your body are no longer affected, therefore you feel loose and stress-free.

This is an effective treatment, but the results are temporary. Once you leave the place and return home, you receive a phone call from work about a project that will be due first thing in the morning instead of next week. Immediately, the tension returns and the problems manifest again. The stress comes back because, once again, your thoughts are centered on the stress and strain of your daily obligations. As you give way to worry and anxiety, the energy center that had been closed reopens, affecting the same areas of your body as before.

Or, say you and your significant other are having issues within your relationship. For the past several years, you have experienced ups and downs. One day your mate calls you on the phone asking for a face-to-face meeting. When your mate arrives at your home, they proceed to tell you, "It's over and I think it best we go our separate ways."

Immediately, you experience a sharp pain in your stomach. It feels as if your stomach is in knots; the feeling is so severe it causes you to become physically ill. Most people can relate to this. I mean, every person knows the feeling of their stomach being in knots.

What's going on? What's causing this sensation? In theory, the tense-shoulders feeling and the stomach-in-knots feeling have similar causes. The difference is that each emotion is attached to a different part of the body, because different emotions activate and deactivate different energy centers.

When we experience fear, a sense of loss and instability, the feelings are often associated with the energy center around the abdomen. This energy center is surrounded by the kidneys, bladder, stomach, uterus and ovaries in women and testes in men. Whenever this energy center is unbalanced and opens to an excessive degree, the excess energy affects these surrounding organs. Issues such as stomach ulcers, acid reflux disease, kidney infections, fibroid tumors, erectile dysfunction and low sperm count have all been linked to this energy center.

When we allow our thoughts to rule us to the point of fear and instability, massive amounts of energy are released in this area, causing us physical pain. Just think about the times you have experienced these emotions, never understanding the impact of your thoughts on your body. The days you spent worrying about things you couldn't control or giving unnecessary attention to impermanent things drained you of energy that could have been used to love God, self and others.

As you walk in the light, you will become aware of your thoughts and how they impact certain parts of your body. Whenever you feel a sensation in a specific part of your body, it is always connected to a thought or an emotion. When you are able to control your thoughts and emotions, you will be able to control your circumstances, as well as your state of consciousness.

Soul Discoveries

As a child, I could never visualize riding my bike without training wheels. They made me feel safe and secure. The thought of not having training wheels on my bike was the farthest thing from my reality. For me, riding my bike with the training wheels was just fine; I was always able to do and go where I desired to go.

I remember the day when the wheels were removed. Dad and I were outside and he told me, "Son, today you will ride your bike without these training wheels. You will be free to do things and make turns you have not been able to make with them on."

Although I was reluctant to fulfill his request, I thought I would give it a try. There he was behind me, running; all along, I was so afraid of what would happen. As I pedaled with all of my might, I looked around for dad and he wasn't there. I was riding without any training wheels! Boy, was I free! Riding that bike without training wheels changed the entire experience for me.

I was able to ride faster, turn quicker, and go places I had previously been unable to go. When you walk in the light, you will begin to experience life through your soul and not your mind. You will experience the spirituality of things in their fullness, instead of being forced to process everything through the mind's limited system of understanding, logic.

When you walk in the light, the soul is freed and it becomes the entity that leads and guides you. You will find yourself making decisions that do not always make sense, but you will be more confident in these decisions. You will pick up on feelings from people whom you do not know. You will feel the vibes and spiritual status of people you once paid no attention to. You will begin to have feelings before things occur, not necessarily knowing what will happen, but having a feeling that something positive or negative is in the air. Certain individuals will enter your heart and mind, and when you call them they will be surprised because when you called, they may have found themselves in need.

You will notice these things because you will be living free of the mind; free of the limitations of logic. You will be just as I was when I rode my bike for the first time without training wheels. You will be able to feel things you have never felt, understand things that once confused you, you will even find yourself becoming inspired to do things you never did before.

This is what true freedom feels like. True freedom cannot be given to any of us by our country, or any country. True freedom cannot be obtained by fighting wars and battles. True freedom is living life with the soul as your guide. It always leads you in the right direction, because its home is your final destination.

Challenge

At this point of your spiritual journey, you are aware of the dark world, you understand how to walk in the light and now, we have just examined things you will come to know and understand as a result of walking in the light. This week, your challenge has two parts. It is important that you participate in both parts and not just one, because together, they will help you discover things about yourself that are necessary for your individual spiritual growth.

For the next week, your challenge is to combine Chapter 2 with Chapter 3. First and foremost, walk in the light at all times. This is done by being intentional with your thoughts and actions, as well as your words. Please review Chapter 2 if you are not completely certain as to what you are to do, because mastery of the steps reviewed therein is fundamental to every other chapter that follows it.

Part 1

As you walk in the light, it is important to be constantly aware of your thoughts, especially the thoughts that keep recurring. Do you find yourself experiencing pangs of jealousy? Do you find yourself experiencing stabs of anger? It is important to really focus on your specific emotions. It's important to know what they are because this will become the map that leads you to your ultimate healing. Think of your thoughts and emotions as clues that point you in the direction of the treasure.

When you are able to identify the recurring thoughts, write them down in your journal. After you write them down, write down any feelings or thoughts you have that are attached to them. Be specific! For example, if your recurring thought is born of anger, I want you to write down what made you angry. Where were you when you became angry? These are important questions to answer in order to resolve the root of your issue.

Part 2

As you walk in the light, it's not only important for you to be attuned to your feelings, but also to the sensations that you experience in your body. When you get angry, what do you feel? When you experience feelings of jealousy, what do you feel? Any sensations that you have in your body, be it in your head, neck, shoulders, stomach, etc., should certainly be written down.

As you progress through this challenge, you will begin to see the correlation between your thoughts and the sensations experienced in your body. All of these are discoveries you will find in the light. This exercise is important because it will ultimately lead you to the change you have always desired, but never knew where to look.

Part I
Betrayal
Taken Advantage of
Guilt of Not Doing Enough / Can't
   Influence

Part II
Heart races
Get hot

Chapter 4

Exploration of a Higher Dimension

The darkness is in my past; the light now leads me. I anticipate all that it brings. My way has never been so clear, my steps have never been so ordered, my posture has never been this confident. I have walked into a new place, one that is higher than where I have come from. I am in a new place and I am in a new season; I am thankful for this chance to make this world a better place. Within me, I will allow my soul to be a permanent place for the light. I will take it everywhere I go. It is my hope that others may grow from what has changed me.

I had good friend who struggled with various issues that were all health-related. He spent a lot of time in and out of hospital rooms. Through the process of being examined by virtually every specialist there is, it was discovered that my friend had a dysfunctional valve in his heart. When told about his condition, the doctors presented him with a list of options in order that he may improve his health and ultimately reverse his condition. The options were as follows:

1.) Change your diet, and begin daily cardiovascular exercise.

2.) Stop smoking and consuming any form of alcohol.

3.) Have surgery, which will repair the dysfunctional valve.

My friend knew his exact condition and issue. He knew what to do to fix it. He was also assigned a trained team of professionals who would help him accomplish those tasks. Less than a year after his diagnosis, my friend was found dead in his home. His weakened heart could no longer sustain his body. He no longer walks among us; however, there are reasons for his tragic end. There are three specific reasons why my friend passed away when he did and they are as follows:

1.) He never changed his diet, neither did he exercise.

2.) He continued to smoke and he continued to consume alcohol.

3.) He refused to have the necessary surgery to repair his heart.

It's one thing to endure certain hardships in life that are unexpected; it's another thing entirely to endure hardships you are fully equipped to avoid. It is my desire that you do not allow the physical fate of my friend to be your spiritual fate. At this point of our journey, you should know exactly what your problem is and how it has affected you, as well as the steps and tools needed to address them. If your walk remains the same, then it means you have decided to maintain your existence in a state of darkness, which will lead to your spiritual demise.

At this point, I must ask the question, "Do you desire to walk in your fullest potential?" If the answer is yes, you must do all that you can to make the adjustments in your life to position yourself to succeed and reach your ultimate goal.

In the previous chapters, you have learned what not to do as well as what you need to do, but what are some specific things you can do in order to make this dream of spiritual enlightenment and growth a reality? In order to accomplish this, it is necessary to explore areas and dimensions that you never have before. If what you have always done has gotten you where you are now, it is only logical that a different destination warrants different actions. This is a wonderful opportunity for you to get to a new place by doing a new thing. By committing yourself to exploring these recommendations, you will be making your first steps in and towards a new dimension.

There are many people in this world who struggle with losing weight. The weight loss industry is a billion dollar industry. Seemingly daily there is a new "secret" to losing weight. There is the South Beach diet, Atkins diet, grapefruit diet, soup diet, liquid diet; the list goes on and on. But what good is a diet if you are not willing to make permanent changes in your lifestyle? If I diet, I will lose weight; but unless I change my lifestyle, all that was lost will be regained.

Your spiritual walk can be understood in these terms. Your walk should not be a temporary one, but rather, it should be a part of your ongoing lifestyle. Life is a journey and it's a journey that requires us to learn something and improve each and everyday. When you read these principles that will help you in your journey, make a vow to practice them daily. If you do, your spiritual growth will take you places you never imagined.

These principles will greatly assist you as you walk in the light. They will be like boosters on the sides of a bicycle, there to help keep the bike upright and moving in the direction the rider points it. You are already going in the right direction; however, these principles will get you there much faster. So what exactly are these principles?

Meditation

Meditation is something that most people have heard about; however most are clueless as to what it is. When the word meditation is mentioned, images of distant eastern religions may dominate our thoughts. In the West, the concept is often considered anti-Christian, against Jesus and it has even been considered "New Age." All of these negative perceptions are nothing but devices people use to further separate humanity.

The reality of meditation is that it belongs to no culture, religion, sect, or group of individuals. Meditation belongs to all of humanity and it is something that will aid any person on their individual spiritual journey. So what exactly is meditation? Meditation is the act of thinking of nothing. It is a readjustment of one's focus from outward to inward. Meditation is the act of silencing all things of the world in order that the voice, sound and direction of the soul may come forth authentically.

I vividly remember, as a child, swimming in the ocean for the very first time. I remember when my father took me out to the sea and held my hand—what an incredible experience. There were fish, creatures and organisms I had never seen before. I saw organisms that were very difficult for me to wrap my mind around. I was seeing a different world, and it was the opposite of the world that I had come to know and understand.

The amazing thing about my experience underwater was that, while there, I never heard any sound nor had any experience that I could relate to life on dry land. I was totally separated from the everyday world. I was in a safe, peaceful and tranquil place that felt so pure and unmolested.

Meditation is very similar to this experience. It is an escape from the world and all things of the world. The stress, hassles, deadlines, problems and issues all leave when we escape into our hidden world. You have a world that is just for you. When you were born, God gave it to you; however, your entire life no one ever took the time to show you how to get there. If you desire to live life to the fullest, it is necessary that you escape to your world each and every day.

When you meditate, you want to find a place where you will not be disturbed, where you can remain alone and in peace. It should be a place where you feel comfortable and safe. When you find the space, select a place on the floor or even in a chair. You want to sit comfortably, close your eyes and let everything go. Remember, this is your world and hidden in your world are the secrets of eternity and the location of your destiny.

As you sit, focus on your breath, inhaling and exhaling. When you first begin, you will notice that many thoughts will rush into your mind: "What do I have to do today? Where am I going tonight? What am I going to eat this morning? What do I want to wear?" These things will recur over and over again.

When you have these thoughts, don't become angry or frustrated. Just understand them. You are having these thoughts because at this point in time, your mind is like a dog that has never been properly trained. It runs recklessly in every direction. It ignores any command of its master. It roams freely, doing as it pleases.

59

The purpose of meditation is to help you train your mind; to put you in control of it instead of it being in control of you

This is the state of your mind at this point. It has its own agenda and it roams your consciousness, freely thinking what it desires, not even knowing that you are its master. It controls you at all times, causing you to become angry when you don't want to be angry. It causes you to lust after others even though you are married. It causes you to do things that satisfy your body even though your soul is compromised by the act.

Remember, you are on a mission and you will not allow anything to prevent you from your goal of spiritual freedom. Every day, you will take time to escape into your world. You may feel that you are getting nowhere, but it is necessary that you continue each day. When you feel those thoughts freely moving through your mind, just regain your focus and return to your breath—inhale and exhale. Each time you find yourself not in control of your thoughts, return to the breath—inhale and exhale. The more you practice this, the more you will become the master of your mind.

As time progresses, you will be able to sit for longer periods of time. You will begin to notice that your thoughts are not controlling you as they once did, but rather, you are controlling them. When you get to the point whereby you are able to sit in silence, thinking of nothing, the magic happens. This is when lift-off begins, and you will find your own world in which you are the only inhabitant.

You will know you are close to this breakthrough point when you find yourself seeing balls of various colored lights. Blues, reds, oranges, violets and golds are very common. Virtually every color of the rainbow can be experienced, and each is special to the state of consciousness that you have at the time. This is the tunnel that will lead you to your soul. This will be the portal of your escape and it's in this place where you will find treasures that this world cannot even understand.

When you find this occurring, do not be afraid, just know God has you and you will be in a place that is free from all things that can harm you. Every sea has different creatures within it and likewise we all have different things in our own world; however, within all of them we will find exactly what we need. Sometimes, you will experience things that cause you fear and pain. You perhaps will experience things about yourself that push you to change who and what you are.

Other times, you may have blissful experiences that leave you full of joy and peace. Whatever you experience, just accept it and learn from it. Know that whatever you experience is what you need.

Meditation is a powerful tool; however, there are some things in this world that can impede or corrupt your growth. Please carefully read my suggestions in order that you do not make a mistake.

1.) Do not do research on meditation without understanding the belief system of the author. There are many people who have written books that contain techniques that may in fact be harmful to your spiritual journey. If you have developed a connection to my words as well as trust in my opinions, there is contact information at the end of the book. You may submit titles that you are curious about, and I will give you my opinion on your selections.

2.) You do not need to say or chant anything— all of what you need is within you right now. Mantras, visuals and other external things are all unnecessary. Remember, focus in on the breath when you sense your thoughts are becoming uncontrollable.

3.) You don't need a guide, guru or teacher to show you how to meditate. God resides within you and He will be your guide.

If you commit to doing this each day, you will discover the difference meditation will make in your life. When you are able to train your mind and what enters it, you will be well on your way. Your spiritual walk will become more interesting because you are able to place yourself in certain states that are more beneficial for you and your journey. Continue daily in your efforts in order that you are not side-tracked. If you follow these guidelines, your life will be greatly impacted.

Diet

The society that we live in now is one that is all about convenience. Likewise, this term has been the motivating force that controls the U.S. food industry. People are steering away from quality and healthiness; they create and purchase things that are fast and cheap and indeed, these foods are killing us.

Many people are familiar with the stunning statistics that reveal how our food is linked to so many health issues, including hypertension, obesity, cancer, diabetes and other illnesses. This is a subject that most people know and understand; however, many of us are clueless as to how the food that we eat impacts our spiritual journey.

In the later chapters of this book we will discuss energy, but allow me to give you an introduction at this point. When God created the world, everything was created from energy and by energy. All matter is comprised of nothing more than units of energy. Although all things are energy, all things have different vibrations or frequencies to them. For example, a piece of sand and a tree are both made of energy; however, they do not have the same rate of vibration or the same frequency.

The frequency of human beings can change instantly. Your mood or emotions often determine your rate of vibration. If you are happy and full of joy, you are vibrating at a higher frequency. Likewise if you are depressed and angry, you are vibrating at a slower or lower frequency. The highest frequency there is, is light. Light is the only thing in this universe that is absolute.

Time is not absolute; it is relative and therefore artificial. Time is something human beings have created in order to make sense of the universe. [1] If you and I were identical twins and I left to travel to outer space in a spaceship the entire time, when I return 10 years later you would have aged more than me. Whenever high-speed travel exists, time slows down, which means time is not absolute.

Although time and space are not absolute, light is. Nothing moves faster than the speed of light. If I am in a jet and you are on the ground and we are both

---

[1] Albert Einstein's Theory of Relativity

looking at the same bolt of lightning, it will appear to move at the same rate from my vantage point as it does from yours, even though I am travelling much faster than you. This shows us that light is absolute and all other things are therefore relative.

What a beautiful understanding. It's beautiful to know that light is the ultimate source that creates, maintains and progresses all things. Light is pure, unrefined energy and I believe the source that gives light its power is the power of God. God made all things in the image of God. From this pure source, you have come. All things come from it; however, in our actions, thoughts and words we dilute it.

Being that light is the ultimate force that all of us come from and the fact that it is the highest frequency, how is it that food or what we eat has anything to do with our spiritual journey or progression? All things come from this pure source; however, when the source becomes contaminated that can change its vibration. Processed food, which is any food that is not in its natural state, such as cookies, bread, pasta, anything in a box etc., have all been contaminated and in many instances their vibrations have been altered. When we eat these foods, their vibratory state will impact ours at the molecular level.

Think about oily skin, eczema, acne, brittle hair, weak nails, painful joints, chronic headaches, weight issues, diabetes or any other health condition you can name. 99% of those issues are directly linked to your diet. Whenever the body does not receive the nutrients that it needs, it is unable to do what it was created to do. The nutrients that the body needs come from energy. A calorie is nothing more than a unit of energy; however, every calorie does not have the same frequency.

Spiritual energy comes from the source and is very light. You have heard the phrase, 'a heavy meal.' While the word 'heavy' generally refers to the amount of food, it also refers to the vibration of the food.[2] The key to linking your diet to your spiritual state is to consume foods that have a lighter frequency. The lighter the frequency, the purer the food. Fruits and vegetables are lighter frequency foods. Specifically, any type of food that is grown in the light, such as mangos, pineapples, oranges, apples etc. are all lighter frequency foods. Vegetables such as leafy greens and various beans are the same.

It's important as you continue on this walk that you make certain changes to your diet. Please adhere to the following recommendations because it will make your journey lighter and easier. As you are making adjustments, it's not necessary to change overnight. However, if you do all that you can to make small changes day by day, within a month's time you will be adjusting at a comfortable rate.

- Always eat whole foods. Whole foods are foods that exist in their natural state and have not been altered or adjusted by human beings. All things in plastic and boxes have been processed, and therefore are not natural foods.

- Increase your water intake to at least 64 ounces of water per day. This will cleanse your body and its vital organs of all toxins. Urine

---

[2] Ed Kuiper, *What's Your Frequency? How to Effectively Use Energy to Powerfully Enhance Every Aspect of Your Life* (Bloomington: Author House). 2007, 47.

should be clear, and if it is not clear it means you are not drinking enough water. The more water you drink, the more your body will release the water that it is holding.

• Reduce meat consumption. Meat is not a high vibrating food. It is a low vibrating food; therefore, the more of it you eat the more it will affect your frequency and vibration. Many eastern gurus will tell you it is necessary to become vegetarian; however, if this is not possible, greatly reduce your meat intake to 1 serving per day.

• Only consume organic produce when possible. When you shop for produce, all organic fruits and vegetables have a bar code that is preceded by a "9." When you see "4," that food has been genetically altered or modified. Organic produce is more expensive; however, the knowledge that you are eating pure foods is worth the price.

• Eat small meals. When you sit and indulge in a meal that has an excessive number of calories, all of the energy your body would use in other places is committed to digesting the food. Remember, when you eat large meals, the body converts the extra calories to fat. "Whenever a meal or snack tops your body's limit of 600 calories in a single sitting, the excess calories—even from fat-free foods—stimulate fat storage rather than fat burning."[3]

---

[3] Robert K. Cooper PhD, *Flip the Switch* (New York: Holtzbrinck Publishers). 2005, 241.

guilty

• Avoid emotional eating. Refrain from an emotional attachment to food. Understand eating is about the transfer of energy. Look upon food as fuel. When your spiritual walk increases, you will have no need to be comforted by food.

• Remove alcohol from your diet. It's full of sugar and it is void of the nutrients that your body needs. If you choose to have an alcoholic beverage, drink red wine, but be certain to limit your consumption of this beverage also.

These steps and recommendations will help you on your spiritual journey. Many blocks that people experience occur as a result of their diet. A good diet, when properly understood, will catapult the spirituality of any individual.

Seek Knowledge

As a child, I thought wisdom and knowledge came by traveling to some distant place in the Far East and visiting a wise old man at the top of a hill. I believed this old wise man would have all the answers to any of life's questions. This myth was and is quite common. What's relevant about the story is not the fact that some old man has all the answers to our questions, but rather that most people believe wisdom is found by way of an outward journey.

The only way wisdom can be found is when we become seekers of truth. The way to obtain truth is by seeking knowledge in all things. When knowledge (mind) is gained, often times it can lead to truth (soul).

Truth can only be found within. If you desire to take this journey, it is necessary that you become a seeker of knowledge. The knowledge that you seek can be found in books, relationships and life experiences. Within each, you will find and learn things that will lead you to truth.

Books

It is necessary to develop a thirst to learn things you do not know. The wise man understands that he knows nothing. When you understand that you do not know anything, you also understand that you are an empty vessel that needs to be filled. There are great lessons that you can learn from books and other resources.

Remember, when you read books, you are not looking for truth in those pages, because truth cannot be found externally. You will find knowledge and wisdom on those pages, which will often lead you to the truth that is within.

One day, I read Albert Einstein's "Theory of Relativity." This theory proves the fact that light is the only absolute because there is nothing that moves faster than light. While reading the explanation of this famous theory, I was able to receive much wisdom by way of scientific discovery; however, after reading and understanding that wisdom, the words resonated with me to the point that I was better able to understand God. Just as Albert Einstein says "light is the only absolute," I was able to have that understanding about God. God or the Supreme Force that governs all things is the only absolute. When we were made in the image of God, we were made from something that is absolute and infinite. Seeking knowledge in books allowed the wisdom that I read to lead me to truth internally.

When you seek knowledge in books, you will find some things you read resonate within your spirit. There will be some things that jump off of the page and glare at you. When this occurs, you know you have come to understand something that will lead you to truth. It jumped off of the page because it was exactly what you needed at the time. The key is to read things you are not familiar with. Don't pick subjects just because you like them, rather, pick things that force you to expand your mind and your consciousness. As you gain knowledge that leads to truth, your consciousness will shift. You will begin to view the world through different lenses.

People

Not only is it possible to gain knowledge and truth from books, it is possible to gain knowledge from people who are in your life. The power of relationships has nothing to do with tenure or time. Many times, we think people we have befriended for 20 years are more important to our growth than the person next to us on an airplane. But remember, time is artificial, it is not absolute; it is only something we humans created in order to make sense of the universe. Every single person who enters your life, be it a lifelong marriage partner or a seatmate on the subway, has been placed there for a purpose. Learn to seek out the knowledge you can gain from every relationship.

In relationships, the process of gaining knowledge that leads to truth happens in two ways. When you meet a person, not only are you to gain something from them, but you are to give something to them as well. Sometimes you can do both and not be aware of what has happened.

Once, I knew a man who was very unique, and whom many would consider strange. He ate by himself and kept to himself, to the point of being antisocial. In car-crazy Atlanta, this man walked everywhere. I would see him every morning on my way to the gym. He would often look at me and likewise I would look at him. I felt a connection to him, but I did not understand why. Being sensitive to the spirit, I acted on my urge and began to converse with him. We spent one hour together each morning for 6 weeks. I learned so much from this man. He was poor, he was not married, he had no children, and he came from a different place than I did, but I was able to gain so much from him.

One day, I shared with him how he had helped me and how he had caused me to learn so many things I was searching for. After I shared my feelings with him, he told me that I did the same thing for him. He said talking to me gave him a confidence that he never knew he had. You see, both of us were feeding and gaining knowledge, which leads to truth by giving and receiving.

In your life, there are people who are around you who have the exact things that you are looking for. They have a word or a story for you that would make all the difference. Perhaps just being in their presence or you in theirs is all that is needed. So many times, we allow the social rules and regulations of the world to disconnect us from finding this truth. We are told to marry people from "good families." We try to surround ourselves with people who are educated and successful. We want to be around people with like interests as well as people with similar belief systems.

Following the ways of the world will not help you find the truth. Truth can only be found within; however, you must learn that others have what you need to lead you to that. Don't pick your associates based on superficial things. Allow your soul and their soul to make that decision. Be sensitive to the feelings that you have when you are in their presence. When you feel things, act on them, because it's your soul's way of leading you. The more you listen the louder it will speak; the more you obey the more direction it will give you.

Experiences

Some of the best lessons you will ever learn in life come from your daily experiences. Wisdom comes by way of experience, and if you are sensitive to your experiences the wisdom gained will lead you to truth. The only way to convert wisdom to truth by way of life experiences is by always looking for the good in all things. Remember, truth is absolute and it is God; therefore, when you have a negative spirit about something you've experienced, you will never be able to let it lead you to the point of gaining truth.

How many times have you ever had a bad day and allowed that bad day to set the tone for the rest of your week, or even month? Have you ever taken the time to say, "What is the meaning of this bad day?" I used to think bad days just randomly happened to me, but as I became a seeker, I realized this was not the case. When I place my hand on a burning stove, there are receptors that tell my brain I need to move my hand or else I will be burned. Sometimes it's easy to focus on the pain of the fire, but when you understand that the pain is a mechanism that keeps you safe, you can rejoice.

In all things that we experience, there are things we are supposed to gain from it. When you experience uncomfortable, painful situations, don't waste time and attention on the pain, but actively look for the lesson you are to gain. From losing your job to the untimely death of a child and everything in between, there is something in the experience that will lead you to truth. When you look for it, you will always find it.

Reflection

The last and perhaps most important step of this chapter is personal reflection. Reflection is the time that you spend reviewing how your actions are affecting your life. Reflection should be done regularly. At the end of every single week, make it a habit to reflect on the last few days. The following questions should be asked:

1.) Have I done my best to walk in the light this week? Have I given attention to my thoughts, actions and words? If I made mistakes, what adjustments can I make in order that I may improve?

2.) What have I gained this week? What has happened that will help me to grow spiritually?

3.) Whose lives have I impacted negatively or positively this week? What adjustments can I make to be more impactful to others?

4.) What areas in my life need more attention in order that I may grow spiritually?

When you include these questions as a part of your reflection, you will always position yourself in a place that makes room for growth, each and every week.

Challenge

This week's challenge is very straightforward and simple. This week you will be creating a roadmap. The road map is a plan that will set you up for starting your journey while implementing these spiritual strategies. The challenge is as follows:

- What time of the day will you commit to daily meditation? Remember, initially this does not have to be a long time. You can start at 10 minutes per day and allow yourself the opportunity to grow from there.

- What adjustments are you willing to make to your diet? What can you change now, what can you change by month's end, what can you change three months from now? The goal is to make all changes so that your new lifestyle reflects what was discussed in this chapter.
- What will be the first book you read on this journey? How much time will you give yourself to finish the book?

- What adjustments can you make in order to more actively seek the meaning and purpose of all persons who enter your life?

- What day of the week will you commit to your fulfilling your personal reflection?

It is necessary that you write all of these answers down. This will allow you to keep a journal as well as keep track of your progress. I am proud of you; you have made great changes in your life and I am excited about the new dimension you will soon experience!

Chapter 5

Between Two Worlds

I'm standing between where I once stood and where I will soon be standing. This is a strange feeling because I have never been in this place. I am preparing to say goodbye to my old home; I anticipate my new residence. I am uncertain as to what the next world has for me, but as long as I remain in the light, I know I will find my way home.

I have been blessed to have some wonderful grandparents in my life. All of my grandparents instilled morals and values in me that I will take and live on for the rest of my life. Today, none of my grandparents are living; however, the things they taught me will live forever!

I remember when my grandfather became ill. He had lived a long life and all of us knew his days were numbered. We did all we could to make him as comfortable as possible to prepare him for his transition. In his final days, I noticed that granddad was acting in a way that, at the time, I thought was weird. He would lie in his bed and fix his eyes on things that we did not see, or scan the room as if he was watching something move around. When we told the doctor what was occurring, the doctor said that this behavior was common for people who were dying. The doctor said granddad was just hallucinating. What he saw was not real, but a figment of his imagination.

I also remember granddad having conversations with people. He would talk and make comments to people as though they were standing in front of him.

We all just ignored the actions assuming that he was just "seeing things" as the doctor told us. But one day I saw my grandfather have a conversation with a person. He was talking to his mother. He gazed, cried and made comments to her that sounded so real, I thought she was really in the room. This scared me because I just did not know what to make of it. I just chalked it up to granddad having one of his moments.

Not long after that, my grandfather passed away. He did not suffer, and he had lived his life as a Christian man who loved others and always tried to do the right thing. I knew he was in heaven and I was able to celebrate his transition.

Now that I am older and I have a better understanding of God, myself and others, I know what granddad was experiencing. He wasn't "hallucinating," and he wasn't merely seeing things that were not there. My granddad was between two worlds. We were witnessing him "crossing over." Granddad was experiencing glimmers of his new home; however, his body still remained on earth.

Dying To Self

The concept of death scares many people. Death, for the most part, is something that most people fear and hope never happens to them. We all know it is on the way, but people do all they can to avoid it. Death is an illusion. It is not the ending of something, it's just a transition or a continuum of life. Energy can never be destroyed or created. When we die, the energy that resides in our body is exchanged to go on to a new place. We merely exist in a different state.

Clean the House

me with God

When we decide to go on this spiritual journey, there must be a type of spiritual death. The only way you can grow and be who and what you desire to be is if the old you dies and the new you is born. The previous four chapters are nothing more than my way of helping you to destroy your old self; the old you that dwelled in anger and rage. The old you that was consumed with sex and addictions. The old you who suffered from low self esteem and the inability to be all you were meant to be. It is my goal to assist you in this, because it is the only way to the other side!

Whenever something dies, the event is surrounded by change. As you know, most of us do not like change. We are creatures of habit and many times we will continue to dwell in a place of familiarity, even when we desire to go to a better place. As you go through this process, you will experience this. You will have moments where you are able to see the new world; however, you will find yourself afraid to continue on to the other side. Don't worry, you have all you need to make it. I believe in you, and for that reason I will help you on this journey. It will not be easy, but when you get to your new home you will be so happy that you did.

At this moment of your journey, you are at your most vulnerable state. You are vulnerable because you do not know anything but what you have known until this point. You have never viewed life from the other side of spiritual freedom and therefore it will feel as if you are going to a place that is foreign. Many people who take this walk fail at this point of their journey. The walk becomes so foreign to them that they give up and revert back to their old habits and actions.

People fail because they are not equipped with the knowledge of what to expect on the journey. Though every person has a different walk, there are some common things that we will all experience. It's important that you push through when you find yourself hitting these walls, because your home is on the other side.

When you are between two worlds, it's important to remember that you are leaving where you have been for a place you have never experienced. This is a very unnerving experience, because your destination is unknown.

I remember when I first went to college. I knew it was where I wanted to go as well as what was best for me, but I was so afraid. What was I afraid of? I was afraid of the unknown. I was afraid of what I did not know. In this journey, you will find that the mind will either be your best friend or your worst enemy. When the mind is forced to participate in something that it cannot understand, it will often justify reasons through logic as to why you should not do it.

The mind has caused many people to miss out on their destiny because it could not understand where they were going. The mind can only perceive two dimensions of time, the present and the past. The mind cannot perceive or understand the future and it is in the future that your destiny rests. On this walk, you will be challenged to do things that the mind cannot understand. For this reason, it is so important that you walk in the light. As you walk in the light, your center becomes motivated by the soul and not the mind. As you continue in this manner, you will not allow the mind's inability to perceive the future to make you hesitate in pursuing what your soul knows is truth.

I shared with you the story of my grandfather's death because a physical death can be compared to a spiritual one. They are similar because in essence, the same process occurs. Something is moving from one state to the next. The process of your spiritual change can be compared to death.

When a person is close to his or her death, there are some signs or symptoms that are very common. These signs are very similar to what you will experience spiritually. Allow each example to be a guide that will prepare you for the journey.

Lack of Energy/ Loss of Interest

As the body nears the time whereby the soul will make its exit, the physical place that has been the soul's temporary home becomes weakened. Muscle begins to shrink and limbs lose their mobility. The body's inability to function as it once did makes everyday tasks like walking, cooking and cleaning a chore and the interest is lost.

Granddad was a gardener. He planted watermelons and collard greens. He grew peas and tomatoes. As a child, I never ate any vegetables that were not grown by the hand of my granddad. I would often see him work in the hot sun all day; it was a joy to him and never a job. He took pride in his efforts. However, as he aged, his body began to deteriorate. The weaker he became, the less he worked in the fields, and the less he did what he once loved because his body was not able to support his interests as it once did.

As you make your commitment to live and walk in the light, keeping watch over your words, thoughts and actions by way of meditation, diet, seeking knowledge and personal reflection, you will begin to change. The old you will start to die and you will notice a loss of interest in things that you once loved. Clubs and partying loses its glimmer. The fast life and those attached to it seem distant. Time spent with family and friends and even alone become states of bliss, not boredom. What's occurring is that your spirit and soul is shedding its former consciousness. You are no longer excited by those things because your consciousness is expanding. You are able to see and experience things that you once were not able to experience.

When I was a kid, I never liked collard greens and corn bread, and pot roast and steak were dishes I never enjoyed. But if you gave me a hotdog alongside a glass of Kool-Aid, I was a happy child! As I got older and went to college, I noticed on trips home that I had a taste for those same foods I once despised. I craved some fresh collard greens and hot corn bread. Today, I never desire hot dogs and the thought of Kool-Aid is repulsive to me. What happened? My tastes changed! They matured and became more open to different offerings. This is what you will experience in your first state between two worlds. You will notice that the things you once liked have lost their taste; therefore you will seek comfort and fun in other activities and with new people.

So many times, people attempt to give up drugs, sex, alcohol and various vices. They give them up and then relapse, weeks and sometimes even days after. This occurs because they are attempting to gain new habits while maintaining the same state of consciousness. This is impossible. If I desire to rid myself authentically of any vices, I have to extinguish the part of me that led me to that behavior. When I destroy the old me, or the old consciousness, I will rid myself of the vice that was connected to that consciousness.

Vices are connected to a particular state of consciousness. All of the things that you do that you wish you could change or the things you do that make you happy are directly connected to your consciousness. It's all connected to the way that you think. For this reason, people are unable to change, even when they desire to do so.

1. Some people lose weight and gain it back, convincing themselves they can never be thin. Their issue is not genetic, but rather it's a question of consciousness. There is something in their consciousness that causes them to seek comfort in food.

2. Drug addicts seek artificial highs for a temporary comfort in a time of pain, then continue to search for that next hit because their desires are connected to their consciousness.

3. The person who is addicted to sex is addicted to it, not because something is wrong with them, but because of their consciousness.

When the consciousness shifts, changes or becomes altered and adjusted through intentional living (e.g. thoughts actions, words), all vices and behavior that are attached to that state will leave and they will not return unless the same consciousness returns. This is key for you to understand.

Your thoughts, words and actions set your consciousness. When you are walking in the light by maintaining positive thoughts, words and acts, you will attract manifestations that are positive: joy, peace and happiness. As you shift your consciousness, the negative vices will literally lose their attachment to your life because those things that you are attracting are manifestations of the light and not the darkness.

There are so many people in the world who suffer from various mental illnesses, addictions and problems. We have been trained to resort to the help of a psychologist when these issues or problems arise. When many people who possess these issues attend sessions with psychologists, the approach of modern psychology is to psychoanalyze the mental state or the mind of the patient. Patients are given tests that analyze how they think and process information. I do believe psychology has its place in the rehabilitation of many people. Still, I think the overall approach of modern psychology is erroneous and I think it often times fails to move patients from their problematic state.

When you look at the origins of the word psychology, you see that in fact, psychology was not always the study of the mind. "The earliest definition of psychology dates back to the 16th century, when the term was coined from the Greek words psyche, or soul, and logos, or study. Psychology then was defined as the 'study of the soul.'" [1] If our desire is to change who we are, we must change that which governs and controls our authentic nature. The key to moving past a certain state of being is to dig deep within the soul. If this is done, change will manifest.

---

[1] Adelaida C. Gines, *General Psychology* (St., Sampaloc Manila, Philippines: Rex Books). 2003, 4.

Loss of Appetite

Another sign of impending death is the loss of one's appetite. When granddad was in the later stages, he had no desire to eat or drink. We all wanted him to eat. It was difficult for us to watch because it was our desire that he remain here with us. Granddad had no need to eat because it was unnecessary to obtain energy from food. He was leaving this place; therefore, he had no use for earthly sustenance.

At age 21, I gave my life to the ministry of others. I knew if I desired to minister to people, I had to make changes in my life. When I began to change, everything around me changed as well. I no longer had the desires to do certain things or go to certain places. The hardest part of my change was losing the people who I considered friends. When they invited me to party, chase girls and stay out late drinking, I didn't want to go. My focus was on something else, something higher than this world.

At that time, I was spiritually enduring what granddad had endured physically. My appetite for the fruits of this world left. My friends reacted to me the way my family members acted toward my granddad. We all wanted granddad to eat so he could remain with us. We all wanted him to maintain his strength so he would stay a bit longer. Likewise, my friends wanted me to continue as my old self. The parties, fast living and all it entailed were the way we bonded with each other. They didn't want me to leave, they wanted me to remain as I once was with them, but I could not do that. I had to journey on to a different place.

Today, as I write this, I want you to know that none of my friends at that time are my friends today. One

People ridiculed my eating habits/schedule because they wanted me to stay the same state as they do

by one, as my journey changed and shifted, they dropped off. The phone calls stopped, as did the emails and the correspondence. We had nothing in common, there was nothing left to explore. I am not angry with them at all; it's just a part of the process of a spiritual death. Many people cannot conceptualize how life would be without the friends that they have now. It isn't the easiest thing to accept, but perhaps if you understand the emotions it will make your journey easier.

Loneliness

As you progress through this stage of your journey, you will experience feelings of loneliness. Your new walk will cause many people around you to directly and indirectly lose connection with you. You will learn in the process the ways you have unhealthily connected with people in the past. You will realize that many of your friendships were based on activities instead of mutual contributions to each other's spiritual progression. When my walk changed and I experienced this state, I learned that most of the friends I held dear were people I partied and did other things with which were not helpful to me at all. I learned in the process that these individuals were not really my friends, but just people who resided with me in the darkness.

You will have this feeling, but know that it is normal. You will feel disconnected from people or the feeling of missing out on things. All of these feelings are completely normal. You are simply caught between where you were and where you are headed. You are trapped between two worlds; however, if you keep moving and pushing forward, you will realize that this state is only temporary.

As I continued to push through this stage of my walk, something very interesting happened to me. Every single relationship I had at the time ended. It was as if I was experiencing a period of cleansing on the inside and on the outside. Remember, when your consciousness shifts so do the things, people and manifestations in and around your life. Once I experienced this cleaning, I saw a new crop of individuals come into my life. Many of these people were already around me; however, initially I had had no interest in them because our interests were different.

This is when your sacrifices will be rewarded. You will experience an influx of new people and new friendships and as they come, all of the feelings of loneliness that you experienced will leave. There is no need to feel bad about the old friends, because it is nothing more than the natural process of a spiritual journey. People come and people go; all persons are planted in and weeded out of our lives for a reason, even the ones that caused us temporary discomfort.

Temptations

As granddad laid on his deathbed preparing to journey to the next life, some days were different than others. Some days he would lay in his bed seemingly in a trance, watching and talking to people who were not there. Whenever he had those episodes he would never eat nor would he drink. Other days, he would interact with family members seated around his bed. He would even desire small amounts of food and drink. What was occurring? Granddad was between two worlds, and in the process of being in-between, sometimes you lean more to one side than the other.

Even though granddad was transitioning, he still had a body, which caused him to live out that reality. As you find yourself in this spiritual state, you will still have temptations of the world. They will continually pull at you, desiring to return you to your old self. You will have days when the drinking and the lifestyle you once had, the promiscuity or the homosexual urges that you once indulged, will find the way back to you. The old self still has some life because you are in the process of destroying it. Even though my Granddad was crossing over, he was still on this earth, which gave him some desire to experience it.

This is the most critical stage of your progression. It is the place where most people become misdirected and ultimately fail. Sometimes the feelings of the old you can be strong and very unpredictable; however, you must remember to maintain your focus and continue to walk in the light. Maintain your positive thinking, continue your positive speech, hold steadfast to your positive actions. If you always revert to the fundamentals that you have learned, you will be successful in your efforts.

The closer my granddad got to his death, the less this capricious behavior occurred. One day, his interactions with us and his desire for food completely ceased. Likewise, if you continue when you feel these urges, they will pass. The struggle you are experiencing is the struggle between the mind and the soul. It is the battle over which one will be your guide. The more you walk in the light as well as practice the other techniques you have learned, the more you will support your soul in its effort to win. The less you do what you have learned, the more susceptible you will be to giving your mind the reins. The choice is yours, but you have been equipped to win the battle!

Transition

The day my Granddad passed away was different from any other day before it. Whereas before he had been caught between two worlds, it was evident in his last moments that he was closer to the other side than he was to this world. Granddad was lifeless, still and his color began to change. His breath began to change. It began to be arrhythmic; sometimes he would breathe and other times he would not. The whimpers and cries of anguished family members streaked around the room, because all who were present knew death was near.

The amazing part of his death is that his countenance was different. Though he had not eaten or drank anything in quite some time and was unable to talk and interact with us, he had a countenance of peace. He was not afraid, nor was he bothered by anything. He could not speak, but it was obvious that he was happy about his destination.

On this spiritual walk, the key to knowing you are almost there is when you receive a peace about everything that you once toiled with. When granddad was between the two worlds, he would vacillate between the two states. He would see visions of people that none of us were able to witness and then he would return to speaking to us just as he had before. Some days he would not want food and other days he would. These actions occurred because granddad was caught up between two opposing places. However, he continued to progress and the closer he got to the new world, the more he gave up his fight for the present one. He let go of everything as if he were welcoming his new destination.

The sign that you are close to a real transition is when you give up the fight. It occurs when you have a peace with all the things you have changed. When the lust for things leaves and the desire to do the things that you once did drifts away in the past. When your new life brings you happiness and does not make you feel as though something is wrong. All of these are nothing more than signs to let you know you are almost there.

Granddad's struggle was only temporary. The time that he was pulled between two worlds, between where he once lived and the place he would soon go, was a short while. I compare this spiritual state to death because they share so many similarities, but there is a major difference. The difference between a physical death and a spiritual death is that we have no choice in the matter of a physical death. Just like my granddad passed away, we must leave this world behind one day. For some of us, it will be years from now, while others may not even see another month. For all I know, I may not even live to finish writing this book. Either way, the point is we do not have a choice.

We do have a choice as it relates to this spiritual death. We have a choice and until you understand the necessity of a spiritual death, it will continue to be something most people try to avoid. Many times as I walk down the streets of my hometown of Atlanta GA, I pay close attention to the health nuts. I admire their hard bodies and their slim, fit waistlines. They walk around without shirts and are able to wear any style of clothing and it all looks great! Boy, wouldn't it be great if we could all have the physical appearance of chiseled Greek gods?

If looking great and having a flat mid-section with an abundance of symmetrical stomach muscles were automatic, we would all have them! But individuals who look like this make great sacrifices to achieve their goals. Sure, some of it is genetic, but most of it comes back to the choices and the decisions that they make. When cookies and cakes are presented, they pass it up. When drinks full of empty calories are served at dinner parties, they opt for water. When the people around them order plates of fatty foods, they choose lean meats and greens. And they make the time to exercise almost every day. Is it a sacrifice? Sure, it is! Is it difficult? Absolutely. Even though it's not easy, it is possible.

This is how you must view your new journey. In order to be who you desire to be, the old you must die! This chapter is nothing more than an explanation of Jesus' conversation with Nicodemus. He said, "Unless you are born again, you shall not see the Kingdom of God." [2] When Jesus uttered these words, Nicodemus was not referring to a physical rebirth, but a spiritual one. He stated exactly what I have tried to explain in this chapter. In order for your rebirth to occur, it is imperative that the old you dies! This chapter simply assists you in that effort.

Isn't it time for a rebirth? Aren't you tired of the life you have lived until this point? Don't you want more out of this life than an abundance of stress and a life full of disappointments? Don't you desire to see things you have never seen and experience things you never thought were possible? Don't you desire to be your best and live your life to the fullest? This will not happen by simply reading a book or going to some

---

[2] John 3:3

seminar. It will only happen when you decide to make this transition.

Challenge

This chapter is the turning point of this book. Not only is it the midway point of this book, but I hope it will also serve as a turning point in your life. There are many things we have reviewed in this chapter. I have told you what to expect and potential pitfalls you will come across. The great thing about this is that at least you know and understand what to expect before it arises.

Your challenge is very simple. I want you to spend some time thinking about the things you need to do in order to complete this process. What is something you need to let go of that you feel will be hard to give up? Is it a certain relationship, activities, habits? Whatever it is, I know you already know it because you are thinking about it right now. It's that thing that seems impossible to give up, but it is not. That's just your mind presenting you with roadblocks to bump you off course.

I want you to write down every emotion that you have surrounding this particular person or situation. How does that person or situation make you feel? What experiences have you had with this person or issue? Whatever thoughts come to you, I want you to write them down. Be as honest with yourself as possible. Know that the more honest you are, the more successful you will be in your efforts to change. Once you have completed your entry, I want you to repeat this empowering message aloud:

I am a new creature. I am more than what I see when I look in the mirror. The darkness has stifled my growth; however, from this day forward it has no place in my life. I vow to always walk in the light. I vow to remain positive in my thoughts, actions and words. What the world has seen from me has not been my best, but from this day forward the world will see a new creature.

My journey will not be easy, but I know I will be successful. I have been destined to succeed, failure is not an option. When I change, I will live my life in order that others may change. I will become a living embodiment of love. Anger, fear and depression will find no home within me. I will make it and nothing will stop my journey. As of this moment, the old me has died. My old thoughts are deceased. My old ways are in the past. My old way of speaking is a distant memory. I am a new creature. I have been born again. From this day forward, I will never be the same!

When you repeat these words, say them with passion. Say them with authority. As you utter them, believe your words. You have come a long way. The old you is in the past, and now it's time to lay the foundations of your future. It is extremely important that all the parts we have discussed be mastered before the next segment of our journey together. If you don't master them, the next section will not yield the desired outcome. Take this time to review any or all chapters in order to prepare for your next experience.

Chapter 6

A New World

As I open my eyes to look at this unknown place, I do not recognize it. I have never seen it before now, but I know this is my home. I am free of my past thoughts, struggles and negative emotions. The slate is clean and my way is now made clear. I have a new guide now: my soul, not my mind. I will live the rest of my days allowing it to lead me to my final destination.

Planet Earth has more than 6 billion people living here. These 6 billion people are different races, cultures, nationalities, ethnicities and religions. We all possess different opinions, thoughts and worldviews; however, there is one thing that we all share. All of us started our journey on this earth as babies.

The day you and I were born, we knew nothing about this world. We didn't know anything about the sun, moon or sky. We didn't have any concept of color or race. We knew nothing of hate or jealousy. All we knew was that what we were witnessing, we had never seen or experienced before. All of the people who watched us, picked us up and fed us were complete strangers.

When our lives began, we had to learn everything that we know today. All thoughts and opinions that we have exist because we were taught to think them, whether we know that or not. Our view of the world, religion, politics and love are all views and opinions we have gained. The things we have learned until this point are responsible for making us who and what we are.

My parents divorced when I was 5 years old. I love both of my parents and I believe that both of them were great parents to and for me. Even though they were great parents, I was still affected by their decision. The point that I wish to make is that all of us are impacted, shaped and molded by things, people, and events that occur around us. There are some things that we create for ourselves, and then again there are things that shape us because we were exposed to them.

As it relates to your journey, you must be mindful of this. You must understand that the people around you, the activities and places you expose your spirit to will all impact your progression as well as your destination. Allow this chapter to serve as a guide to show what you should focus on in order to be successful in your efforts. I won't be able to show you every possibility, because your journey is different from mine and we all have different experiences. What I will share with you are the things I have learned from my journey. It is my desire to share with you the things I learned on my journey, in order that you may learn as well.

What's In Your Diet?

The best way to look at the New World is through the lens of a newborn baby. It's the best way to view the place because that's exactly what you are. You are new to the environment and everything that you experience is a new experience to a certain degree. A child growing from birth to maturity takes time, effort and a plan. Every newborn baby needs certain things in order that that process is complete. Allow this to be your framework of understanding.

When a child is born, the most important factor in the child's proper growth and development is nutrition. The child has been in a place whereby he is surrounded by darkness within his mother's womb. Though he is able to receive nutrients and sustenance, he has never been in a place whereby he has had to do anything in order to receive his nutrients. When child is in his mother's womb, whatever she eats is the foundation of his nutrients. Therefore, if her diet is full of vitamins and minerals, he will receive them. Likewise, if her diet is poor in vitamins and minerals, he will be absent of his basic nutritional needs.

Until this point, the world has been the womb that has fed you. You have been nourished by the elements of your surroundings. This means that your nutrition from the world comes from circumstances you have experienced. Many people have been fed an abundant amount of anger, fear and distrust. Your life has been full of doubt and anguish and you have been fed by those experiences. For this reason you see how your life largely has been a reflection of the suffering you have experienced.

Many times when someone is raised in an environment where violence, hate and loneliness are states of normalcy, they have been literally nourished by this atmosphere. Whatever we eat is what we become and this example is no different for many of us. When we are exposed to the things of this world, we become fed by them as well.

As the child who is raised in anger and fear grows, he becomes that pain. As he matures, he begins to issue to others what has become a part of him. He will raise his children in many of the ways he was raised.

His understanding of love will be corrupted because he only expresses love as he experienced it.

The point I desire to make to you is this: Before we became "born again," the world was the womb that provided us our nourishment. But remember, you are no longer connected to the umbilical cord of the world. The old you is now dead and the new you has been born! The principles are the same in this place, yet the source whereby your nutrition comes is different.

When children are born, there are an abundance of supplies that can be purchased from local marts and grocery stores to make feeding faster and more efficient. There is cow's milk, baby food, Similac and like products that are said to provide a child's fundamental nutritional needs; however, statistics have all shown that children who are healthier and often times smarter are the ones who have been breastfed.

Children who are breastfed get everything they need because all that they ingest comes from their own source of origin—their mother. Now that you have entered the new world, the source of your nutrients has shifted. No longer will you receive your nutrients from the world, but rather from the authentic source you came from—God, the Light, the Supreme Force that governs all things. This will be your source that gives you all you need. It has all you need because you are an extension of it. You were made in its image and therefore you will never be in a position whereby you are unable to get what it is that you need.

When we remain connected to the source, all of the needed nutrients and energy are given to us, allowing us to be strong and focused on our journey. As you enter this new world, you will have a different impact on people. This impact on people will occur because now you are a clear reflection of light. The old you is deceased and in the past, and the new you has been born again.

Like Moths to a Flame

The presence of goodness, love and joy will be a part of the spiritual experience that people observe from you when they are in your presence. As a child, I spent many summer nights in Georgia. I remember listening to the loud echoes of the night owls and the crickets. Whenever I would go outside, I always noticed the many different types of bugs that would hover and land on various light posts. The light attracted them from all points. It seems to me that light is a universal element that all living things need and desire to be exposed to.

When babies enter this world physically, everyone is universally attracted to them. People want to hold them and care for them. People want to be in their presence, to look at them and be close to them. What is it that people are attracted to? People are attracted to the innocence of that child.

Their purity—people are attracted to their light! When we are newborns, we are more authentic than at any other time in our life. We are sinless, without fault. We have no understanding of race, color and socio-economic status. We do not hate, we are not judgmental—we are pure reflections of light. It's when we grow that the light that was once the focus of our identity is dimmed.

When you enter the new world , people will be drawn to you just as they are to a newborn baby, and just how those summer bugs are drawn to the light of the summer night. People will be attracted to your light; however, many of them will not even understand why they are drawn to you. Within you, they see something familiar, yet they are unaware of what it is. Allow me to give you a few examples of things you might experience now that you have arrived in the new world.

1.) One day you are walking down the street and you notice a person staring at you. You are unaware of why they are looking at you; however, it is obvious they are looking at you. They approach you and begin to speak. They ask you questions and you respond. The moment feels so random that both of you may walk away feeling confused. What happened? Your light attracted a person—it's not a physical attraction, but a spiritual one. Most times we confuse these experiences, but now you will be aware of them.

2.) At work, you notice that every time anyone has an issue, they approach you to talk about it. You find yourself counseling so many people, it's almost as if you have become the unofficial counselor of your division. What is it about you that's so great? Why do people openly trust you to share their innermost secrets? It's your light. What summer bugs see in the lamp light and people see in newborns is the same thing others see in you. As your journey continues and grows, the more attractive you will become; however, there is a danger that you need to know and understand before it occurs.

The purpose of this segment is to teach you to remain connected to the source at all times! What's the source? The source is God, the Supreme Being, and the state that contains all things good and positive. What's attracting so many to you is the light that you get from this source. When you walk in the light by remaining in tune with your thoughts, actions and words, your spiritual reserves become full of this light. Staying connected to the source does the same thing for us that the charger does for our BlackBerrys and our iPhones. It causes us to be full and when we are full we are able to function and operate at the height of our abilities.

When you arrive in the new world, you must do all that you can to remain CONNECTED to the source. If you do not, your light will fade. Your power will cease. Your ability to connect with your soul will become impaired. This is the key to your success. So how is this state of our lives a potentially dangerous place?

When you are a reflection of light people are drawn to you, and you must remember they want what you have. This is not similar to a thief desiring to steal or to take something from a victim, but rather is like a bug on the light post. Just watch their behavior—they will hover and land on the light post. They don't do anything to it or with it—it's as if they are drawing from the energy of that light. When people see you, they are drawn to your energy! Often times they are unaware of it but they want it. They want it because they come from it just like you do.

When people come to you and are exposed to your light and energy, they will pull from you. They will take that energy because it makes them feel better. When people are with you they leave feeling uplifted and better about themselves and their life. Many times they are completely ignorant to this and they will sometimes reduce how you make them feel to simply "liking you." It's much deeper than that; when they are in your presence they draw from and take your light. How can this happen?

1.) Spiritually toxic environments: Clubs, bars and certain parties are major venues whereby your light can be drained. You must understand we are porous creatures. This means we are constantly emitting and receiving energy. When you are in places like this, you will have feelings of fear, depression and anxiety. The feelings you are experiencing stem from your light being drained and contaminated.

2.) Negative, draining people: There are many people in your life who you will recognize as "light leechers." Whenever they come around, you experience feelings of negativity and spiritual and emotional taxation. The emotions that you feel once again are the effects of your light being sapped from you. You must learn how to share your light in order that others may be changed; however, you cannot let your light be stolen from you. This occurs by altering your relationships with certain people. If there are people in your life who fit this criterion, you must change the way you interact with them. Your time with them cannot be for pleasure or to pass time, but rather it must be to give them direction and point them on the right path. When you are using your light in this fashion, it will be for the good of others, which will enhance and expand the light that all people see and experience.

3.) Uncommitted, lustful sex and masturbation: Sex was given to humankind as a gift. It is the vehicle of life as well as the way spirits connect and bond together. When we participate in sex, our bodies expend the energy that it takes for that physical experience. When you have sex with a mate, the energies are balanced because the spirits are like and are communicating in a dimension that is not of this world. When we participate in sex with people whom we are not spiritually connected to, the person with a lower vibrating frequency of energy will pull from the person with the higher vibrating frequency.

Likewise with masturbation, the results are the same. In this situation, we are draining ourselves of our own light. Whenever we participate in masturbation, the mind is the conduit that allows us to pleasure ourselves. In essence, a spiritual encounter takes places in the mind. When people masturbate, energies are expended, but there is no other soul present to counter and refuel the spiritual conduit of the giver. Therefore, energy is lost and light becomes drained. For this reason, many people who masturbate afterwards feel dirty, lonely and depressed. These feelings are in direct connection to the spirit's loss of power, energy and light.

Staying Filled

Being that you are a reflection of this light and a bearer of the light, others will seek you out and desire to obtain what you have, so it is imperative that you always remain connected to the light. Imagine a large barrel that is full of water. As long as the barrel is whole, the water remains. However, imagine if we were to drill one, two, or maybe even three large holes in the bottom and sides of the barrel. Upon doing that, the water would precipitously exit the bottom of the barrel. In a short while, the barrel would be empty of water.

This is how you must view your life from this point forward. We are vessels that hold and retain light, yet there are instances that occur on a daily basis that will drain us of this light. Like the barrel, the struggles and strains of daily living create holes in our spiritual vessels. Habits, stress, unhealthy environments and negative relationships are all examples of the holes in our vessels. These are the things that drain us of light.

Remember the example of the barrel? Well, imagine that same barrel with leaking holes on the side and on the bottom being filled by a continual supply of water. Just think of this barrel being positioned underneath a waterfall. The beauty of this image is this: as long as the water fills the barrel more quickly than it exits, then the barrel never loses its state of fullness.

Likewise, you must look upon yourself as this barrel. There will be events and people that drain us of our light, and to a large degree that is okay. There are times when sharing your light with others is needed and necessary. For example:

1.) There will be times when it is necessary for you to shed light and love on people who do not love you in return. Maybe you work with someone who's mean to you for no good reason. You may be uncomfortable, but that's okay because you are bringing light to places where there was formerly only darkness.

2.) There will be times when you need to bear the burdens of others, even though they have created their problems themselves. Perhaps you are called to help the homeless. Even though some people become homeless through the choice to abuse drugs and alcohol, your role is still to assist them.

3.) There will be times when you are treated unfairly by others or perhaps placed in unhealthy environments that are no fault of your own. Those who have experienced abuse and neglect were put in these horrible environments and forced to carry those burdens.

All of these things will happen to you and you should expect them, and to a certain degree, it's okay. However, you must remember to remain connected to that waterfall—the endless abundance of pure light that constantly fills you. This is the reason for our thoughts, actions and words always being as they should. When my thoughts, actions and words remain in the light, it means I keep that constant flow of energy within my vessel. Your meditation, diet, personal reflection and the seeking of knowledge are all ways that will help you to stay connected to the light on your journey.

If you decide not to abide by this most important rule, there will be consequences. Besides being an author, I am also an active pastor of two churches in the Atlanta area; thousands of people worship in the churches I have been planted at week after week. As a pastor, I am nothing more than a vessel of light, used to shed that light onto the people who seek it. Being in ministry, I am constantly giving light to others. I prepare all week long, sometimes spending 40 hours for one 45-minute message. I prepare Bible studies, counsel those in need, officiate funerals and weddings and I am always listening to the stories and pain of those whom I serve.

All of these acts constitute a few of the holes in my barrel. Although I am a bearer of the gospel and the act of teaching others is a great thing, it is still a process or an act that bleeds me of light. Sometimes I feel as if there are thousands of holes in my barrel, and there have been times when I have been guilty of not staying connected to the source, that endless flow of pure power and light. The reason I am able to teach you this is because I have lived it. I know what it feels like as well as what happens when we lose our connection to the source.

In my life, whenever the holes of ministry bled me of my light and I stayed disconnected from the source, terrible things happened. Understand this: Even when we lose the light that is within us, we are still vessels. If a barrel is not full of water, that doesn't negate the fact that it's still a barrel. All it means is that the barrel is not being used properly. When we lose our light, we still have purpose, integrity and even a certain amount of usability; we are just rendered ineffective.

If you were to take that barrel away from the waterfall and randomly place it, say, under a group of trees, the barrel would still be a vessel as it was before; however, it would be filled by something other than water. It would become filled with dust, dirt, and dead leaves. Animals would make a home of it, animal droppings and straw and other debris would fill it. After all of the debris fills the barrel, the dirt and matter would decay, becoming a paste of sorts that would seal up the holes. At that moment, the contents of the barrel are nothing more than debris that is stagnant and unable to move on.

This is what happens when we are not connected to the source. We become full of mess that stops us up and causes us to be vessels that are unable to be filled. Whenever in my past I have not maintained my connection to the source, this is what happens. Debris would seep into my consciousness. The lowest points of my life have been after times when I shared my light with others. When I refused to maintain my connection to the source, debris would enter my consciousness.

Anger: Anger would often times present itself in my vessel when I would neglect to reconnect to the source. I was full of anger at times. I would become impatient and upset at the least little thing. I would be angry with things that were small and relatively insignificant. I often reflected on how strange my actions were. Here I was a pastor, a man of God, but I was acting like a devil. I had issues within my consciousness that were totally against what I knew was right. What was happening? My barrel had been removed from the waterfall.

Pride: Pride often times presented itself in my vessel. After ministering to thousands of people, after witnessing masses of people crying and emotionally moved, people who took every word I said as the truth and nothing but the truth, the old me would feel I was responsible for that. My ego would grow and I would feel as if I were something special and different. My interactions with people changed and became altered because I was viewing reality through blurred lenses. The truth of the matter is, I was nothing more than the barrel. The water that seeps from that barrel actually comes from the waterfall—it only appears to be coming from the barrel because it moves through it. My pride prevented me from seeing that all things within me were coming from the source. It was the light, not me. What was happening? My barrel had been removed from the waterfall.

Lustful thoughts: Many times after sessions of ministry, where I would share my light with others, I noticed immediately afterwards that my mind would travel to places that were not of the light. Thoughts of lust, sex and physical indulgences would consume my consciousness. Initially, I ignored the thoughts, praying they would leave; however, the more time passed, the stronger my desire to act on those thoughts became.

I wish I could tell you I was able to resist them, but I cannot. So many times, I found myself in environments whereby my soul was compromised by the desire to fulfill my flesh. Here I was, a man who chose to live his life helping others and showing them the light and the importance of establishing a relationship with God. Yet here I was, living a life of deviancy. I found myself all alone. I did not know what to do or what to say. Did I have a problem, was something wrong with me, did I need help? I could never answer these questions. Now that I am past that distant point of my life, I am able to understand my state of mind, and I am able to share it with you. What was happening? My barrel had been removed from the waterfall.

Today, I can tell you I have been delivered from that. I do not have the same issues that I once did. My deliverance resided in my ability to understand the power of the light as well as the need to always stay connected to the source. I took the source for granted.

I felt that all I had to do was give to others, yet, I wouldn't take the time to replace what I was giving out.

There have been many instances of members of the clergy and other spiritual and religious organizations falling to the fruits of this world. Sex, alcohol and drugs are often connected to members of the spiritual and religious communities. Why is that? Why are these scandalous occurrences so common? They are common because individuals in those positions are constantly sharing their light, as well as being constantly drained of their light. Many of them never take the time to reconnect to the source. They remove the barrel from the waterfall and it becomes full of debris: pornography, acts of homosexuality, drug addictions and alcohol abuse. None of these actions are reflections of their character. They have simply removed the barrel from the waterfall.

How Do I Remain Connected to the Source?

1.) Always walk in the light. Each and every day, hour, minute and second of your life, spend it watching and observing your thoughts, actions and your words. This cannot be expressed enough. You must retain positive thoughts that are of the light. Always monitor your words. Never allow any negative, pessimistic or degrading words to ever exit your lips. If you are properly mastering your thoughts, you will be able to effectively monitor your words. Finally, always make sure your actions are in line with your thoughts and your words. Allow your actions to be such that your light is on display. Allow your actions with others to be rooted in love and service to those who are in need. Allow your actions to be selfless. Allow you actions to be the very essence of the light.

2.) Always keep with you the fundamental tools that allow you to walk in the light: meditation, proper diet, the seeking of knowledge and finally, personal reflection. These tools are not a stand-in for walking in the light; they are merely exercises to help you on your journey.

3.) Surround yourself with people who are light bearers as well. When you expose yourself constantly to those who walk in the darkness, they will drain you of your light; however, if you expose yourself to those who walk in the light, you will be positively affected by their walk as well. Imagine one mirror in a semi-darkened room; the mirror is unable to reflect much light. However, in a room full of mirrors the light is exponentially illuminated. When you surround yourself with other light bearers, you will be in an atmosphere that is full of light.

How Often Should I Connect to the Source?

I knew a man once who lost 200 lbs in 15 months. He lost the weight by eating less than 20 grams of carbohydrates per day. Just as a point of reference, one regular bagel has approximately 38 grams of carbs. So for 15 months he ate half the carbs found in one bagel. Even though this seems excessive, it worked for him!

Soon after he had met his goal, someone asked whether he would return to his previous diet of bread, pastas and other high-carb foods. He responded by saying, "The last 15 months of my life was not a diet, but a lifestyle change."

As it relates to your spiritual walk, this attitude must be permanent. This must be a lifestyle change for you. If you look upon this as a temporary state of existence, it will only be a matter of time before you return to your original state of darkness. The source must be with you at all times and in all facets of your existence. When the source is always with you and connected to you, you will always be full of those things that you wish to live, think, know and see.

What Causes Disconnection from the Source?

You are the only thing that keeps you from the source. Many times, it seems as if the people around us, places we visit and the activities we participate in are the culprit; however, this is nothing more than an illusion. You are what keeps you connected to the source. For this reason, you must always live your life with a sense of intention.

This chapter is such an important part of your journey. It's so important because this is the chapter that helps you to lay the foundation of what is to come. If you are able to realize that the key to all things rests within your ability to connect to the source, you will never, ever, at any point of your life be without anything. The source is endless. It will always be there for you. It will always provide for all of your needs, even when you don't know what they are.

Please heed these words and take them with you for the rest of your life. When you walk in the light and remain connected to the source, it is impossible for you or anyone else to take you away from where you should be. Life and the world will look so different and your eyes will be able to behold all of that you have missed.

Challenge

Now that you have made it to a new world with a new consciousness, it is time to think about your future and what you desire to see in it. What are your new goals and aspirations? What do you choose to do with this new life that you have brought about?

Years ago when I was at this point of my journey, my desires changed. I noticed that my desire for things of this world lessened. I am not saying they disappeared completely, or claiming that I will never buy things of this world, because I like a nice pair of shoes just like the next person! I guess what I mean is, my desire to covet those things has left me. They are of no value to me. This is how you know change has truly occurred in your life. When I changed, I had strong desires to share my light with all who would allow me the opportunity to share it with them.

When my prayers and desires to share the light became my goals, doors opened that allowed me to do that. Opportunities beyond my wildest dreams have been presented· to me and everything I do has been successful. I do not say this to boast or to brag but to merely show you that when you are walking in the light and you remain connected to the source, your life becomes authentic. When you are led by your soul and not by your mind, you see things clearly. You will naturally steer away from things that are not for you and you will naturally gravitate towards other things that have your name on them. I am excited for you, but we must set your vision!

This week you will have challenge questions. Take some time and internalize each question. Write your answers in your journal.

1.) What are you looking to get or gain from your life in this new world?

he

2.) What goals do you wish to accomplish?

3.) Are there any fears or anxieties that you possess about this new stage of your life? If so, you'll find information at the end of this book which will allow you to contact me in order that I may assist you through this period.

4.) How do you plan on staying connected to the source? Even if your answers are more than what I have suggested, feel free to write them down. Spirituality is a personal walk, which means your walk may be different from my own.

I hope you feel proud of where you are. I am so proud of your progression and I am so excited about what I will share with you in the next chapters. Take this time to review all aspects of what you have read. It is necessary that we continue to build upon what we have learned.

1. a. Intimate Relationship w/ God
   b. greater discernment
   c. healthier/slimmer body — off all medication
   d. opportunities to share about the Journey
   e. successful/profitable business w/ my cards
   f. abundance of God's favor & His finances in my life — ultimately to be a giver and to be debtfree

2. ALL The above

3.

4. To live the way God wants me to — totally dependent on Him Continue to grow stronger & be more consistent with my meditation

Chapter 7

The 4th Dimension

The place I now find myself in is indeed real; however, there are so many things for me to learn about it. My senses have become altered; I see things I used to overlook. I have emotions for people and experiences that are new for me. Life is more purposeful and colorful. My way feels as if it has a new meaning. I do not understand this place, but I look forward to what the new day will bring.

The chapter you are preparing to read is perhaps going to be the most difficult to comprehend, in many ways. I will do my very best to explain the new state you now find yourself in, assuming that you have followed the contents and suggestions of each chapter prior to this one.

If you read this chapter slowly and carefully, you will learn many things that will improve the life you now live. You will receive insight and guidance on things that are necessary for your journey.

Just for a brief moment, I want you to use the wonderful imagination I am certain you have. Just for this chapter, I want you to imagine that the world we live in right now is a world of two dimensions. As you know, the world that we live in is 3-dimensional. A 3D world simply means that the things we interact with and the things that we see in this world come in three measurable dimensions, which are length, width and depth.

All things that we see fit in these measurable dimensions: trees, hotdogs, bicycles, fish, horses, you and I are all 3-dimensional. Everything in this world, from the fundamental building block, the atom, all the way to the Great Wall of China, has a measurable length, width and depth. These measurable dimensions make the planet that we live on a 3-dimensional place.

For the sake of this chapter, I want you to imagine that instead of a 3-dimensional world, we instead live in a 2-dimensional world. Let's assume that, instead of all things residing in the three measurable dimensions of length, width and depth, all things reside in just the two dimensions of length and width. In this world, nothing has any depth to it.

If the world were really only 2D, all things would appear flat. They would only take up space that could be measured by length or width. It's hard for any of us to imagine this, because even when looking at a television or a painting, human beings understand the real world as a place of three dimensions, and therefore see flat 2D surfaces as appearing to possess 3D images. This occurs because there are principles such as perspective, shadowing and certain technologies that add the illusion of depth, which artists and movie technicians use in order to give the appearance of 3D. However, when you look closely at the screen, you see it's flat; just the images appear to be 3-dimensional. With me so far?

Ok, back to our imaginary 2D world. Remember, you and I and all we know to be real have only two dimensions. Our homes, cars, clothes, churches and even the food we eat can only be measured in 2 dimensions; all things, for lack of a better word, are flat! For the sake of imagination, let's call our new 2D world, "The Flats."

Let's say that you and I, as well as the rest of the people who reside in The Flats, are at our community gathering place and we are having a cook-out. We are cooking flat hot dogs and flat hamburgers. Our kids are throwing flat balls and we are drinking flat drinks! Lol, the point is, all things are flat, and nothing has depth to it, because all things in The Flats are what? You've got it—flat!

In the middle of the day, while all inhabitants of The Flats are outside in our flat 2D world, out of nowhere a 3-dimensional object hovers above us. We all collectively look up at it at the same time. You must remember, our world is 2D and here we are looking at something 3D. Not only is this object measurable in length and width, but it has something about it that is totally different from anything any person has ever seen. This new strange object has depth as well!

Wow!! All of us are amazed and shocked. We don't know what to say, do or even how to respond. For the first time in the history of our flat 2D world, we are looking at something that is 3D. If this occurred, what would we see? How would we feel?

1.) First of all, none of us would be able to accurately describe what we saw. Why not? Because it is very difficult to explain something that you do not understand. The best any of us could describe this object would be to say, "It's weird."

2.) We would only be able to comprehend the parts of the new object that resided within the 2D world that we understand. The concept of depth is foreign; therefore we would not be able to fully comprehend what we were seeing. All we would be able to say about it is that it's different.

3.) Many of us would become fearful and scared. We would not know whether this object would harm us or not. We would have these feelings because it would be outside our realm of experience.

As you know, everything that exists in our current world today is 3D. All things can be measured by length, width and depth. But what if all of us gathered in a real park, and were grilling our 3D hot dogs and hamburgers. Our children are throwing their 3D balls and we are having some 3D drinks. What if, while this was occurring, something that contained four dimensions hovered about us for the first time? What would we see? How would we feel?

1.) First of all, none of us would be able to accurately describe what we saw. Why not? Because it is very difficult to explain something that you do not understand. The best way any of us could describe this object would be to say, "It's weird."

2.) We would only be able to comprehend the parts of the new object that resided within the 3D world that we understand. The concept of a measurement beyond length, width and depth is foreign to us; therefore we would not be able to fully comprehend what we were seeing. All we would be able to say about it is that it's different.

3.) Many of us would become fearful and scared. We would not know if this object was something that would harm us. We would have these feelings because it would be outside our realm of experience.

If you have precisely followed the instructions of each chapter up to this point and you can honestly say you have made the necessary adjustments I have recommended for you, I can say today, "Welcome to the Fourth Dimension!"

What is a dimension? A dimension has nothing to do with a logistical place, but rather it is a state of being, awareness or consciousness. Dimensions transcend time and space, which means you can physically live where you have always lived, yet you can experience different dimensions according to a few things you will soon learn.

As I told you at the beginning of this chapter, this is perhaps the most difficult chapter to grasp because the subject matter is something that is quite different from what we know and understand. However, it is my belief that you will gain much knowledge here which will help you on your journey.

When I say fourth dimension, it is necessary that you understand what I am referring to. If you do research on the fourth dimension, you will find a lot of information that has its foundation in science and physics. This fourth dimension is a bit different from what I mean when I use the phrase fourth dimension, yet there are some similarities as it relates to the basic function of a dimension. So, if you research the fourth dimension in other books and reference materials, please be clear that I am not talking about the same state or point of existence, yet you will see some similarities.

As I said earlier, the fourth dimension is a state of being, awareness or consciousness. If you have been diligent in carrying out what you have learned in the previous chapters, you are entering this state. The fourth dimension is a special place because your physical body has no abilities to know, understand or navigate it. It is a different dimension because it is a state whereby your soul is able to exist. You must remember, we are spirits that have physical bodies wrapped around us. When you understand this, you will understand that as long as we live on this earth, we will have experiences on both planes and dimensions.

Many of us do not understand this, because we have been taught that only things in the physical earthly setting are real. We have been trained in our schools, communities, families and cultures that only things of this physical world are real. When a person is taught that, they will accept it as truth. The person will only give awareness to those things that are of this physical world. Therefore, dreams, visions, spirits and other realities of the fourth dimension will be ignored by the person. The person has the natural ability to reside in both dimensions, because we are all physical and spiritual beings, yet the person will blindly follow the only one that he accepts—the physical world.

At this time, some lights should be going off for you. You should be gaining awareness about your journey that you did not have before this point. You remember in previous chapters, I told you that the process of dying to your old self brings a new consciousness or awareness. I told you that when this occurs and when we authentically change, we become "re-centered." The process of being re-centered means that the soul takes the lead and the mind becomes secondary. This is key to this transition. This is the reason you are entering the fourth dimension.

You are in this place because your soul is now your center. No longer is it your mind. You are being lead by your authentic self, yet you logistically remain in the same physical place. It sounds weird and strange, but it's very true and you must grasp this in order to receive total understanding.

By making this change, you will have new experiences and new feelings throughout your life and consciousness. This is the case because your soul now allows you fresh views on your life, God, people, relationships and even decisions that you have never before been aware of. You will feel totally connected to God. The voice of God will be so much clearer because you are now in a dimension that allows you direct access to your creator, without the dense 3D interference that you lived with before this point.

Before I get into the actual explanation of the fourth dimension, allow me to reference Jesus Christ. In one of the earlier chapters, I quoted a conversation Jesus had with Nicodemus in John 3. Nicodemus came to Jesus one night and asked him about his talents and gifts. When Nicodemus asked Jesus this question, Jesus responded by saying, "Unless a man is born again, he shall not see the Kingdom of Heaven." This is the foundation of understanding the fourth dimension. Jesus is saying to the man, only if you are reborn (spiritual) or the old you dies to yourself (spiritual), then and only then will you see the kingdom of heaven.

Jesus is describing a dimension; Jesus is describing a place that transcends time and space. You are here now (in the fourth dimension) because you have been reborn. You are now functioning in a place you have not been trained or taught to understand. Though the soul does not need to be trained, it does need guidance at times.

Life will be so very different for you now that you have been re-centered. Now that you have been re-centered, you are able to witness and see the kingdom of heaven! Isn't that beautiful, aren't you glad to know that all of your sacrificing will allow you the opportunity to see and experience something so beautiful? You will soon learn that what you have given up is worth what you will now experience.

God's kingdom is here and you will see it while being on earth. I will explain to you how this works so the revelation I received as a result of residing in the kingdom of heaven may assist you on your journey. Much of what I share with you will not be documented. I have no way of getting other writers' books and resources to prove that what I tell you is real or true—those are functions of the mind. What I share with you is true because I have experienced it. Much of what is shared here I am not certain why I understand it as I do, but I am positive that what I share is real.

How does the 4th Dimension work?

In this universe that all of us find ourselves in, we must understand that all things are made of and sustained by energy. This energy manifests itself on several different levels. Forms such as light, electricity, kinetic, heat and chemical energy are just a few examples of how energy can manifest itself. "An important scientific discovery in the 19th century was that energy is conserved. This means that energy can be converted from one form to another form but the total amount of energy must remain the same."[1]

Energy is what allows all things to maintain their individual existence in the universe. We also know that all matter is made from the same fundamental building block, which is an atom. The next time you go to your home or the place where you live, pay attention to the bricks or slabs of wood used to frame the building. Those bricks or wooden slabs are the building blocks of your home. They are the fundamental pieces used to create the entire home or apartment.

As it relates to all forms of matter, we know that the fundamental building block for all things is the atom. The atom is a microscopic particle that has three components. The core is made up of a proton and neutron and there is an orbiting subatomic particle called an electron that circles around the core, similar to the way the earth orbits the sun.

Please take a moment to think about that—all things are made of the same thing! That's pretty interesting, isn't it? Well, if all things are made from the same thing, then what makes cats different from dogs, or a chair different from a sheet of metal, or me different from you?? Good question, isn't it? In the answer, we will learn one of the key pieces to our spiritual puzzle.

---

[1] G.M. McCracken and Peter E. Stott, *Fusion: The Energy of the Universe* (Burlington: Elsevier Academic Press) 2005. 7.

What separates all things, despite them being made and created from the same fundamental building block, is its vibration or frequency. A vibration or frequency is nothing more than how something responds to or is affected by energy. Let's say you and I are driving down the road and we are in your car. Say you desire to listen to some jazz but I want to listen to some blues. If we turn to a certain radio station that plays your favorite, jazz, then it means we must set the dial or the station to a specific channel. The channel that we tune into is a "radio station." A radio station is nothing more than a device that interprets a certain frequency of energy and transmits that wave that it is sending to your car—and there you are, enjoying the sounds of smooth jazz.

After we listen to your jazz station for 30 minutes, being the kind and considerate person you are, you allow me to listen to some good ol' fashioned down home blues! In order for us to do that, we cannot leave the radio on the same station; we must turn it if we desire to listen to blues. The frequency we are on now is only able to interpret the radio waves of the jazz station. If we desire to hear the blues station, we must turn to another radio station.

The blues radio station has a certain number, or name. Perhaps 94.6 WBLZ or 760 AM, whatever the known station for blues is, this is the one we must turn to in order to listen to the blues.

The station that we turn to simply allows the radio to interpret the waves that are being cast from that station. Radio waves are nothing more than energy that is projected through the air. The radio is a device that reads or interprets those waves. The various channels on a radio allow me to listen to my desire station.

Every radio station that you listen to acts in a similar way, but it is only able to interpret the waves that are sent out on the same frequency it is on. If you understand this, you will understand why all things are different even though all things are created from the same fundamental building blocks. All things respond differently to energy, just as radio stations do. Their response is different because each is on or has a different frequency. Your frequency, or however you respond to energy, is what allows you to experience what it is that you experience.

Consciousness or awareness is about frequency, or how each individual responds to energy. You will only experience those things that are synonymous with the frequency you are on. Applying this analogy to the conversation between Jesus and Nicodemus, we can paraphrase as follows, using our new understanding of energy and frequency:

Until a person is changed (born again), whereby his frequency matches the same frequency of God, he will not see the kingdom of heaven.

Ladies and gentlemen, this is the key. A higher consciousness and the fourth dimension are about changing our frequency. When we change our frequency to one that transcends the 3D world we physically live in, we are able to see, hear and experience things that others are unable to see, hear and experience.

Energy and frequency is a real event that occurs each and every day. There have even been times when you noticed the frequency of other people; however, you did not pay attention to what you experienced. There was a time in my life when I made frequent weekend stops at the same mall. The mall I visited was considered "the spot," or the place to be. Wherever you are in the world, I am certain you have a place like that near you.

This was the happening place because it was where all "the cool people" went to shop and hang out. The mall was one of high profile celebrities and high-end shops. It would be filled with successful, affluent, attractive people and there was just something about the place that I enjoyed.

As I continued to progress spiritually in my life, I continued to go to this mall; however, my experiences changed as time passed by. One day, I entered the mall and felt a physical sensation on, in and around my body. The energy of that place was overwhelming and I had to leave immediately! When I left that day, I never returned for years afterward. The only reason I returned was for a brief visit to a specific store; however, the times of hanging out there were over. What occurred?

In the days before my spiritual transformation, my frequency was very different than it is now. I was able to be part of something that obviously my spirit and soul received and acknowledged. I was able to be part of the energy of my surroundings. It was a part of me and I was a part of it. What happened that squelched my desire to return?

When I was transformed, my spiritual frequency changed. My response to energy was different. I was like a radio station that had been changed from jazz to blues. I was no longer able to interpret and understand the same frequencies of the old me. This is what happens to us every day. Now that you are operating at a higher level of consciousness and now that you are in the fourth dimension, you must understand this.

Anytime you go to a place, or are confronted with a person, or attend an event and you have a feeling of discomfort, uneasiness or the like, it is caused by an energetic opposition of exposed frequency. What does that mean? Your spiritual consciousness is being inundated by a frequency that it does not understand and that it is unable to interpret.

When you and I were driving in the car and we were turning from your jazz station to my blues station, a few clicks before my blues station, we heard a lot of static. We were very close to it; however, we could hear nothing but static. This is what happens to us spiritually. When you are in environments whereby the frequency that you are emitting is different from the frequency of your surroundings, there is a clash or static of sorts. The two forms of energy are repelling one another. It's similar to oil and water being forced to mix with each other—it does not happen. So what can we learn from this?

The lesson that we can learn from this is not to ask when have I experienced this clash, but more so when have I not experienced this. The reason this is the preferred question is because the theory works in the same fashion when applied in the adverse way. Let's say, for instance, that I go to a place that is not consistent with the light, or that I do something that is not of the light, or I think something that is not recognized by the light and it feels okay, normal and there is no objection. This means whatever I have thought, done or said is on a frequency that is a part of me. This means I am that and there is no objection from within my consciousness.

This is an excellent litmus test because it tells you the frequency you are on. Whatever you can participate in without a feeling of conflict means you are doing something that is of or on the same frequency you are emitting. When I traveled to that mall and felt the way I did, there was a conflict that occurred within my consciousness. It was my soul's way of letting me know I was in an environment that was not consistent with anything it knew or understood.

What you are learning are the rules of the fourth dimension. These are the types of things you must know and understand in order to progress on your journey. No longer are you a spiritual being only exposed to a physical reality. Instead, you are a spiritual being, aware of the fact that you are a creature like the Na'vi in the movie *Avatar*. You are a soul that is wrapped in a covering called a body. Now that you have become re-centered, you are able to experience a level of consciousness you have never experienced before. Allow this chapter to lay the foundation of your understanding of this new dimension.

Expectations of the 4ᵗʰ Dimension

Communication

All human beings possess a mind, body and soul. As discussed earlier, each entity has a different duty or job for this journey. The soul is the essence of our being. It is the source of who and what we are. The soul has nothing to do with personality—many people believe this is the case, but it is not. Personality is formed and shaped through the experiences of life, good and bad. The essence of who we are is the soul.

The body is the vessel that allows us to experience a physical reality. It has no other job but that. It is a casing, a shell, a type of container for something far more precious than itself. It is relatively valueless; however, it is needed for our journey. We are unable to learn in this physical reality without it; therefore, it is necessary that we care for it in order that its early demise is not the reason that the soul is unable to learn what it needs to on this journey.

The mind is nothing more than the brains of the operation. The mind is the computer that allows us to run and function, rather like in today's cars. The brain is not the engine, but the instrument that allows things to happen and to occur. The mind should always be the assistant of the soul; it should never be its master.

When we want to communicate with other people, there are a few ways or methods to do so. These include talking, writing letters, composing emails, sending text messages, video conferences, etc. Most communications consist of one of the above-mentioned formats. This is a fairly common occurrence in the physical world. Although these are common ways to communicate, the fourth dimension allows human beings ways of communication that are far superior to what we have mentioned.

The fourth dimension is a place where the soul and other non-physical entities reside. The fourth dimension has a different frequency from the 3D reality to which we are accustomed. The way energy works and travels in the fourth dimension is very different from what we know in physical reality. The fourth dimension is thought-sensitive.

Communication does not only occur when a person sends a text, email or makes a phone call. Instead, human souls and spirits communicate in this dimension all the time by way of thought, emotions and feelings. When souls and spirits communicate, technology is not needed; phones, emails, and text messages are not needed. Time and space are not needed. The person does not have to know or understand a specific language or slang. It is something that occurs at a rate that is faster than any speed we have ever been able to see.

Every time I find myself in a bind, in danger or perhaps just in an uncomfortable life situation, my mother will call me and tell me "You were on my mind, son." Sometimes she will be even more direct and ask, "Joseph, what is wrong, my son?"

There were times when these phone calls would startle and surprise me; however, I am able to understand them now. My soul actually communicates with my mother's and hers with mine in this dimension. This happens all of the time to billions and billions of spirits each and every day, yet we are unaware of it because we are not able to tap into that frequency.

I have felt strong sensations from certain people that are deposited in my spirit. I sometimes feel sensations throughout my body, in my stomach or side, my neck or perhaps even on or around my head. There have been times when these feelings occur that certain people come to mind and I am aware that they are in need. Sometimes their need is major, and then again, sometimes they are just in need of a familiar voice.

It is said that husbands and wives or couples who enter parenthood together will often times feel the pains of the other person. Men will even have symptoms and child bearing pains of their wives or significant others. This is something that has happened since the beginning of time; however, we just chalk it up as folklore or superstition. The reality of what I share with you is the presence of this higher dimension. This is a realm that is above what and where we live now. Souls and spirits interact in this space. Sometimes this occurs between people who know and other times when they are not aware of it.

Now that you are residing in this new dimension of reality, you will have deeper experiences with what I have shared with you. Many people experience these feelings and sensations; however, they are afraid of them. They have feelings, sensations, visions and even dreams of things that are happening, yet they ignore them or are fearful of them. The best way to move past this is to understand that it is okay. Whatever comes to you is something you need to know and understand. Do not be afraid to embrace what your soul tells you. Accept it and know it is of the light. Please allow the following suggestions to help you navigate through this period of your journey.

1.) If and when you experience these strange feelings, hear voices and or see visions, understand that what you hear, see or observe is not something of this physical world or reality. If you have a vision or a thought of a car crashing or a plane falling or a person being punished or abused, it is not always meant to be taken literally. The higher dimension is a realm that is above this world and you must understand this. The more it happens, the more you will understand what I mean. When things come to you, listen to them and attempt to receive them. Don't worry about understanding them, because the need to understand something is a desire of the mind, not the soul. Accept it and know it is real and it is something you need to know.

2.) If what you come to know is about a specific person, do not tell them what you see or what it is that you know unless you are positive it is your duty to share those words with them. Whenever there is doubt, it means certainty does not exist. Only speak and share something when you know it is your duty to do so. How do you know the time is right to share what you know? You will know, the soul will never lie to you or guide you in the wrong direction.

3.) As time progresses and you remain on the frequency of this higher dimension, your abilities will increase and become more powerful. The visions and voices heard will become more vivid and apparent. Your ability to know what is occurring as well as the significance of the experiences will be that much more obvious.

4.) Initially, you will notice that many of the feelings that you have will be related to people you know or perhaps those who are close to you. People such as your parents, children, significant others—these are the most common; however, as time progresses, you will begin to have experiences with people that you do not know. You will have feelings about people before they enter your life. You will receive revelational knowledge about the lives of others.

5.) The moment you use any of what you've experienced for self-gain or for the acclaim of others, the experience will become distorted. The dimension you have now attached yourself to only understands and interprets elements of the soul. It only knows and understands things that are from and of God.

6.) Keep all of your experiences to yourself. No one else was made to receive what you have experienced. When you share with people things that were not meant for them to receive, you potentially alter the maturity of the experience. When people give you their opinions or feedback on the things that you share, often times it will interfere with your authentic understanding of it. The soul needs no assistance besides the guides that have been given to you. Unless you know within your spirit that you are to share what you have received with a person specifically, keep it to yourself. As you continue down this journey, you will understand these words.

Five years ago, in a hotel room in Chicago, Ill., I found myself completely unable to move. A sharp pain was in the lower right side of my back. It felt as if a person was trying to get my attention by poking me in the back. Shortly after this sensation, I observed a scene taking place before my eyes.

It is very difficult to explain because what I saw was in a higher dimension. Even though I could not explain what I saw, I noticed one person in this vision was someone very close to me. I could not make sense of what I saw, because the vision was not a chronological linear vision. It was a series of scenes and images that made no sense to me.

As soon as I was able to move I called the person that I knew in this vision and I shared with them everything that I saw. When I shared with them what I saw, everything that I said made sense to them and was of great significance. Even though it made no sense to me, the person understood exactly what appeared to be a crazy occurrence to me.

The person I shared my vision with was in the midst of seeking revenge for something that had been done to them. What I saw was exactly what the person had been thinking and planning. When I shared with the person what I saw, the plan was ceased and a peaceful retreat was made. This is what happens when you walk in the light. When you walk in the light and your consciousness expands, you are able to communicate and have experiences that are above this physical reality. As you continue on your journey, you will have experiences similar to what I have shared. You will experience things that are far beyond anything you have ever experienced.

Transfer of Power

Earlier in this chapter, I shared with you what we learned from Albert Einstein. We have learned that energy is conserved, which means it is neither created nor is it destroyed. Energy and the amount of energy that something possesses is the key to life and death. If something contains too much energy, it will not be able to sustain existence in its current state. Its molecular structure will change. It's similar to placing a fresh egg in boiling water for 15 minutes. After the time has elapsed, you still have an egg; however, its molecular structure has been completely changed. Energy, in the form of heat, changed the egg. Whenever something is exposed to energy, it changes. It never remains the same.

Believe it or not, your current state at this very moment in time has everything to do with your exposure to energy. If you are feeling down and depressed, it is because you have lower levels of energy. At this time, you have learned a myriad of different things that could possibly contribute to your state, yet at this point of the journey it is important that you understand it is a matter of your exposure to energy.

Now that you reside in the fourth dimension, you are more than a mere bystander and observer of events in the fourth dimension; you now have the ability to control and manipulate power and energy for the edification of people, your community and all humankind. In the New Testament, it talks of what I share with you. In Acts Chapter 2, God gave humankind the ability to harness and control power. This power in the New Testament is called the "Holy Spirit." Some reference it as the Holy Ghost. I call it energy.

The Holy Ghost is nothing less than the pure presence of the almighty God. It is the light; it's the same source that created all things in the Old Testament, or what some scientists refer to as the author of the big bang. Many say that the big bang was an expansion of light or energy. Either way, all forms are the same.

At this point of your walk, you must understand the fact that you are a person who is able to manipulate energy. Because you are walking in the light, the energy of the light is affecting your mind, body and soul just like the heat from the water affects the egg.

Your mind is affected by the light, because now it has been positioned to be a supplement and not the main engine or source of your consciousness. The mind is made a slave to you, not you a slave to it. Your thoughts are controlled and constant. You are able to focus your thoughts and direct them toward areas that will be positive and assist you and others in their walk. No longer will your thoughts be like an untrained dog running wild day by day; rather, they will be channeled according to your will.

Your body will be affected by the light because you are now giving it what it needs to run efficiently and effectively. Your joint and muscle aches of the past will dissipate, because you are not inundating your body with abundant amounts of food and toxic sugar. Your portions are controlled and the emotional attachment that you once shared with food is now a distant memory. Your consumption of low vibratory meat has decreased, and your increase of high vibratory plants and fruits are raising the level of energy your body is able to receive.

Your bowels are now more effective and pass your food as it was designed to. You will find yourself having the need to eliminate several times a day instead of once a day or less. Your skin will clear up; your hair and nails will become strong. Excessive amounts of weight will fall away, your sleep will improve. Medications you were once prescribed will be unnecessary as your health improves. Your sleep will improve and be interrupted less. Your sexual vitality will become enhanced because your complete body is affected by energy. You will be living exactly as you were designed to exist.

Your soul will be affected by the energy. It will be like a caught fish that is released to its home. As the fish is placed in its familiar environment, the water will fill its gills and energy will return to it, allowing it to be free and react in a state of authenticity. The soul is at home now. It has all that it needs and therefore it is able to be your guide throughout this journey. The only things that will be important to you are those things that it has attachments to: things that are on a frequency it can understand and interpret.

Physical beauty, status, race, religion, culture and gender are all forms the soul is unable to understand and interpret. It will only be drawn to the things that are on its frequency. It will only respond to love in all of its forms. Whenever it is presented with a vibration that is not of love, you will know. It will notify you just like an alarm when an intruder has trespassed. You will have feelings and sensations throughout your body notifying you of this. Your soul is different now, because it has been affected by energy.

So how are you able to transfer this power?

Power can be transferred at any time; however, your ability to transfer this power is not limited to one form. Just like every part of your being, mind, body and soul has been affected by energy, you will have the ability to transfer power from each entity at will.

Mind

The fourth dimension, as explained earlier, is a place of higher dimensional spirits and energy. Every thought you possess has attached to it a certain vibration. Thoughts are nothing more than forms of energy. For this reason, our thoughts do lead us to certain physical manifestations. We cannot see this taking place in the 3D world that we physically live in; however, every thought you possess turns into something, whether we accept this or not.

The frequency of our thoughts dictate the frequency of what is manifested. If my thoughts are ill and depressing, more than likely this is what I will experience. This is a fundamental law of nature. It has its roots in agriculture. If I plant a tomato seed, I will grow a tomato. If I plant a watermelon seed, I will grow a watermelon. I am quite certain you get the point. Thoughts are seeds that grow into whatever it is that was planted. For this reason, you see now why your thoughts, words, and actions should always be of the light. If you do as you have learned, your life will change because you are planting new seeds.

Now that you are in this higher dimension with an expanded consciousness, you will be able to control and transfer your power to others for their well-being and edification. This can be done by using a few thoughts.

1.) Whenever you take time to focus on a particular person and their well-being, in essence you are transferring energy that is inside of you to them. There is much power in this exercise. Sometimes it is exactly what others need to make it through their hard times. We live in a world whereby we are so consumed with ourselves that we never take time to practice this; yet there is great power in this exercise. Get in the habit of transferring your energy to those who are in need. There is nothing that is said or done, but just the fact that you think of them and envision them being delivered from their current situation plants the seeds that will often times bring joy, peace and happiness to their lives.

2.) When you are around people whom you wish to help, set up time to spend with them in private. When you sit with them, it isn't always necessary to say things or do anything. Just sit with them in silence, focusing your thoughts on their well-being. When this is done, you will notice a bond is developed between you and them. You will find yourself thinking of them more often and feeling a sense of connectedness to them. The bond that is made is above this 3D physical reality; you have bonded with them in a higher dimension.

The foundation of what I have explained to you is the fundamental reason why prayer really does make a difference. It makes a difference, yet all individuals are not successful in their prayers. Why is it that some prayers are answered and others are not? The answer comes back to where the prayer comes from. Our society has taught us that prayer is about what we say and how eloquent we can be. We are taught to be fervent and serious in our prayers, which does have some validity, yet is not what causes prayer to be powerful.

The power of the prayer is about the origin of the prayer. Does the prayer come from the mind, or is it birthed from the soul? When we pray from our souls, we literally control the energy current of that prayer. When you pray from your soul, the mind is not in play. The mind is what corrupts our prayers and oftentimes destroys the seed before it is planted. The mind will often dismiss the knowledge given by the soul, because the mind doesn't believe the soul's messages. It doesn't believe them because the mind is governed by logic.

If I am praying for a person who has a terminal illness and the doctors say the prognosis is dim, if the prayer of healing comes from my mind, it will be difficult to accept. The mind will automatically process the fact that the person has a statistical disadvantage against him, therefore as the prayers leave, they leave tainted and broken. The seed that is planted is not one of expectation, but of doubt.

When prayers come from the soul and the situation is the same, it yields a different outcome. When prayers are about the soul's energy and not the words of the mouth, the seed is whole. The seed is whole because the soul doesn't need a prognosis or a diagnosis to affect it. The soul doesn't look upon the expectations of doctors and medicine as a point of reference, because it interprets all things on a level that is above this 3D physical reality. The soul knows and understands the fact that all things are possible, so as the prayer leaves the soul, it leaves with a sense of certainty.

It leaves knowing and understanding that this energy that is being emitted will plant the seed of change. This is what makes prayer so powerful. When people gather together and pray for one person for one reason authentically, all of their energy currents are released into the higher dimension, sewing seeds that can change the course of any person. Have you ever received a blessing that you knew you did not deserve? Have you ever been delivered from something that should have you in its grasp to this very day? This happens because someone around you thought of you and prayed for you. Someone released a seed that you are now harvesting.

Body

It is also possible for you to transfer energy from your physical body to the physical bodies of others. There is a beautiful story of Jesus Christ being touched by a woman who had been sick for a very long time. When she touched the hem of his garment, she was healed. Jesus knew she has been healed because he exclaimed, "Someone touched me." He knew this because he felt power depart from him.[2]

This story is a great example of power or energy being transferred from one person to the next. Many do not understand or accept this, but it is real. What makes this possible has nothing to do with what is said, done, studied or even the environment. It has everything to do with the contents of the vessel. It has everything to do with the person being one who walks in the light.

Do you remember the illustration in Chapter 6 of the barrel under that endless waterfall? As long as it is connected to that waterfall, it has something to share with and give unto others; however, when the barrel is moved, it becomes full of debris. When you are

---

[2] Matthew 9:20-22 NIV Translation

walking in the light, energy encompasses your total being. Your cells and atoms are different because they have been affected by the energy and light that you are constantly exposed to.

When you find others who are in need of your light, give it to them. It is very important that you listen to the following suggestions when you attempt this. If and when you have located a person who is need of your assistance, this should be your approach.

1.) Before you began your session with them, prepare yourself. You should be abiding in all of what you have learned. You should be spiritually cleansed and existing on a plane that is higher than this physical reality. If you have read all chapters before this point, you should know exactly what is necessary to achieve this. If you are not prepared as a vessel, there will be nothing to transfer. If you are not walking in the light and your barrel is not connected to that endless supply of energy, you will have nothing to give.

2.) Get the individual to tell you specifically what is wrong. Get them to tell you what hurts or what needs attention. Allow them to talk uninterrupted and closely listen to every word that is shared. As you listen, your soul will began to talk with you. It may tell you things that may deviate from this list, but whatever it says, listen to it and do it.

3.) Start off by holding their hand in silence. Focus your energy and your thoughts on that person. Envision yourself shedding light and thoughts of healing and deliverance upon their life. Don't get caught up in saying certain words, just allow whatever is in your soul to come forth authentically. I am a Christian and I have accepted a life that is devoted to Christ. Sometimes I pray in the name of Christ and other times my focus is on Christ. Allow your thoughts to be yours. Allow your soul to lead you and guide you to say or do what you feel at that moment. Whatever comes to your consciousness, it is important to act on it. This is your soul guiding you to the needs of the person. Sometimes the words that come to you are exactly what the other person needs at that time.

4.) After you have taken time to focus your thoughts and focus your soul on the person, allow your hand to be guided toward the places that need attention. If it's their head or back or arms or foot, wherever the area is, don't be afraid to move your hands on the point. Focus on that area. Envision the pain and disease being lifted from the body. Envision healing and positive manifestation from above being transferred to this area.

5.) After the session has ended, remember, it is now time for you to recharge and reconnect to the source. Energy has been removed and power from within you has been directed to other places. Be certain to resume your habits as you did before, in order to refill you with energy that has been passed.

Soul

We have examined how the mind and body can transfer power; now let us take some time with the soul. We are living in times whereby the cost of energy is at an all time high. Corporations as well as independent inventors are doing as much as they can to increase our abilities to harness, control and use various forms of energy. One of the most common forms of energy now being used in private households is solar energy.

Large solar panels are installed on the tops and sides of homes. When the sun is up, these panels are designed to capture its energy and store it in certain cells, to be used to power the various electrical devices of the household. The technology known as solar power is based on concepts that are very similar to how you now function.

You are now living and existing in a higher dimension. Energy will radiate from you at all times. It will radiate from you mentally and physically. Spiritually, it is no different. Every time you are in the presence of others, this light and energy will radiate from your mere presence. The key to your ability to transfer power from your soul to others will be the capstone of this entire book. Understanding this will lead to your ultimate purpose as you take this spiritual journey. Your ability to be as the sun and give light to those around you will be the very reason why you are able to help and assist others. Allow this brief segment to be a foundation for your understanding of this later chapter. I will reference this when it is time for us to explore that part of our journey together.

Challenge

At this part of your journey, you should have a totally different view of life. Things are different for you now because your consciousness has expanded. This expanded consciousness gives you have a broader awareness of all things. Allow this challenge to be an exercise that brings you full circle to your new spiritual state of being.

We all have people in our lives who need change or help in their situations. Some people need money, while other problems cannot be fixed by a dollar amount. Either way, you are now in a position to help them with your ability to transfer power and energy. Pick a person in or around your life who is in need of help and assistance. Follow these three suggestions as you familiarize yourself with your new abilities that exist within this higher dimension.

1.) Select the person and write down their name and their issue.

2.) Spend the next week making them and their issue your focus. Use all of what you have learned and devote all of your energies and focus on them. Allow this to be part of your meditation; be certain to give them the attention you would give yourself.

3.) After the week has ended, ask if you can meet with them in person. Tell them you just want to spend time with them alone. Take them through the steps that we reviewed.

4.) Before, during and after the events, journal all emotions and feelings you experience while preparing for this event.

This event will change your life if you closely follow what you have been taught. Not only will you see the person and their current state uplifted, you will also discover many things about your personal spiritual life that you have never known before this point.

*********** **Important Note** ***********

Remember, after these events, it is necessary that you replace what was expended. Remember to closely abide by the principles that you learned in the earlier chapters. If you do this, you will be able to keep that connection to the source!

Chapter 8

Empty Space / Shadows on the Wall

*I reside in a new place that is empty and blank. It is pure
and unmolested. As I stare at this place, I wonder what I
should do with it. Do I bring something to it, or should I just
stay here enjoying it for what it is? For whatever reason, I
feel that this space will remain in this state until I change it.
Whatever I place where I reside will be full of light. I come
from the darkness and I will never return to that place
again. My current state may be void of what I once knew to
be reality, yet I am glad that the darkness has been
removed forever.*

Several years ago, a game called "Sims" was released
for various gaming systems. The game gained much
popularity because it was something that had never
been seen on the gaming scene before. The point of the
game was to create, build and organize a city or
community of people. The gamer was in complete
control of the look, actions, living status, location and
daily routines of the characters created.

The game was a huge success because people, for
the most part, enjoy participating in things that lend
them full power and control. The game was quite
amusing. Just to play something that allows you the
ability to do whatever you desire was fun to me. It gave
you the opportunity to see how well your creations work
as well as how they are able to interact with one
another.

At this stage of your journey, you can be compared to
a person who is playing the game I just mentioned. At
this point, you have made several changes and
adjustments in your life. You have been reborn and you
now find yourself in a position where the slate is clean

and the space is empty. You are now the author and the creator of many of the things you will experience from this time forward.

There are certain people who will read what I have written and have issues with my statement. It may seem as if my words suggest that we as human beings create our future and destiny. Allow me to explain exactly what I mean in order that we may be clear. Do we as human beings create our future as well as lay the road to our destiny? Yes and no; allow me to explain.

As stated earlier, I am a Christian and I believe and accept the teachings of Jesus Christ. There are times that my thoughts and opinions may be expressed a bit differently than "traditional Christian thought;" however, the foundation of my faith is rooted in the life, death and resurrection of Jesus Christ.

That said, I do believe in divine intervention in the lives of human beings. I believe God interacts with us as we are on this spiritual journey. I believe God intervenes in our lives for a myriad of reasons. A few reasons are as follows:

1.) Direction: I believe God sends people into our lives that are designed to lead and guide us while we are on this journey. As stated earlier, the soul does not need or use logic; however, it does need guidance at times. I believe God sends these guides in the forms of other humans, angels and spirits.

2.) Provision: I believe there are times when God provides for us when we are in need. I have experienced the hand of God in this form in my life on several occasions.

3.) Divine Intervention: I believe there are times in our lives when God intervenes to change or alter a course that has been determined by decisions and life circumstances.

I want to make it clear that I do believe and accept that God makes contributions to our present and future in many ways; however, I also believe we play a part in that construction, as well.

One of the gifts that we as human beings have is something called free will, or choice. You and I have the ability to choose any and everything we do. We can choose what we eat, where we go, and what we think, say and do. All of these are examples of our ability to pick and choose.

The creation of evil was for this purpose. Good and evil both existing at the same time gives human beings the ability to choose. If good existed without evil, there would not be any such thing as choice or free will.

This concept means that we as human beings are co-creators, to a certain degree, of our future. We have some say and control over what occurs to us. For this reason, as we learn to live life with more intent, we are learning to create or influence our lives positively. Walking in the light allows you to fashion your future and the things that manifest in your life.

It is important to understand that, as we walk in the light and live our lives with more intention, it does not mean that the manifestations we bring to our journey will necessarily affect our circumstances. Doing these things doesn't stop or change what happens around you. Please don't assume that life will become easy, effortless or without struggle or adversity; this is not what is affected. Struggles and hardships will be a part of life for as long as any of us live, yet, the way you live impacts your perspective of those circumstances.

Happiness, joy and peace rest within your ability to shift perspective of your circumstances. It has nothing to do with them, but rather, how you look at them. Your conscience is, in essence, your perspective. It is the mechanism that allows you to see and understand the world as you do. Before your transformation, your perspective was limited. It was limited because everything you experienced revolved around logic and the interpretations your logical mind was able to assume from your circumstances.

When a person becomes unemployed, logic can move you to a state of panic. Your perspective revolves around being without. Logic tells you that you have no job and no income and therefore it is a good possibility that you will go without food, the lifestyle you are accustomed to or even the ability to sustain your home. As long as you are led by logic, this is what you will experience because it understands nothing above and beyond what it sees.

When a person loses a loved one, logic can cause them to reach deep states of depression. Logic causes them to focus on the loss of the physical relationship. Logic causes them to feel that they will never talk to, see or feel the other person again. Logic causes them to make an attachment to the body lying in the coffin. Logic causes them to feel that the sum of the deceased one's existence is the physical life that was lived. The person sees and experiences these things because the mechanism that leads them is affecting their ability to perceive.

When you become re-centered, as we have, the game of life becomes different. Circumstances will often remain the same; however, your view of them is altered. Have you ever purchased a new car (or one new to you), and noticed afterward that you see that specific model everywhere? This happens often. When we buy something that becomes a part of us, to a certain degree, we began to notice it more than we once did.

What happens that causes us to experience this? Do people go out in a mad rush to buy the same car you now own? Of course not! When you decided to make that car a part of your daily life, it changed your perspective. When you leave your house, you subconsciously notice what has become a part of you.

When you understand this, you will see how your new walk will change your life. Your new commitment to change and become a new person has nothing to do with eliminating certain circumstances from your life; however, your point of view will be altered. This shift in consciousness and perspective is what gives you the new experiences. An altered state of consciousness means I do not view the loss of my job as the end of the world. I view it as a part or piece of this journey. By viewing it as a part of this journey, I am able to have a different experience at this time of my life.

My view of the entire situation becomes bigger than my employment status, and I am able to observe and experience things I would have missed. Perhaps I can concentrate on certain lessons that I experience while in that state. Perhaps while unemployed, I meet people who will sow seeds in my life and I in theirs. Perhaps the time that I spend away from work allows me to receive some form of knowledge or epiphany that causes me to become even more empowered than the person I was before. This is how a shifted perspective works.

When loved ones leave me, I am not absent of emotions, yet I am able to view their deaths differently. I now have an expanded consciousness that allows me access and understand dimensions that are higher than my own. I now understand that the soul is an immortal entity that can never die or be destroyed. Understanding this fact causes me to disconnect my emotional attachment from the physical form of the loved one.

It isn't necessary for me to make quarterly trips to the graveyard, because my attachment to my loved ones is not constrained by time or space. They are a part of me forever because our spirits have merged. I may not see them with my physical eyes, but I know they are with me. Certain signs and clues that occur and happen to me day by day give me comfort. I will see certain flashes of light or strange animals that look at me in odd ways. Perhaps the wind blows a certain way, or while I am walking to and from my daily obligations I get feelings of peace and comfort.

Does this take away the fact that the person has died a physical death? No it doesn't; however, their death does not rob me of my ability to connect with them. My expanded consciousness allows me to see above my circumstances, giving me the ability to connect with them for an eternity.

So now that you have a shifted perspective and an expanded consciousness, what is the next step? Now that you understand that you are a co-creator of things that you experience, by the fact that you have free choice, what will you do now? The real question is, what will you place in this empty space? In essence you have taken all known things and you have emptied them. Spiritually, you live in an empty place that is void of your past. The slate is clean and blank, and everything that you see on the inside of the space will be what you place there.

At this time, it is important that we position the right things in this space. You have a choice. The first option is to live the rest of your life free of the darkness and all the things that plagued you in that state. You have a new view of life, and that within itself will be enough to keep you in a constant state of happiness, joy and peace. You interact with people differently than you once did; their opinions of you no longer affect your state of joy and peace. Or you have a choice to put something in this empty space.

You have a choice to not only raise and change your own situation, but you have the choice to change the world. You have the choice to really make this place better than it was when you found it. You have all the tools; you have been equipped. We have been on this journey together step by step. You are reading my words because one day I had to make the decision to fill my empty space. I had to make a choice to use my new tools to plant in the lives of others. I wanted my journey to allow me to help others with theirs. I wanted to be a light that allowed others to see their way more clearly.

I could have been content with my empty space. I could have lived the rest of my days content with my new view of life, but that is not what my life or your life is all about. We were not given the opportunity to learn on this journey simply for our own edification.

We were given this opportunity in order that we may influence others to change along with us.

In the movie, *I Am Legend,* Will Smith's character tells the story of an assassination attempt on reggae superstar Bob Marley. Gunmen wounded him days before he was scheduled to perform at a peace concert. The people around him assumed he did not want to go forward with the performance, but when asked if he wanted to cancel the concert, he told them no. His profound reasoning was that people who live to make the world a bad place aren't taking any days off, so he wouldn't take a break from doing all he could to make it better.

Wow! What a statement, what a way to view this life. At this point of your journey, it's not about you, it's about others. Let's fill this empty space. On gravestones, the entirety of your life is represented with a dash between the year you were born and the year you die. When our lives end, let's have lived in such a way that people see the dash and associate it with how we affected the lives of others.

The foundation of filling this empty space revolves around finding your purpose. Purpose is a term that has been overused, to a large degree. It is a term that many desire to understand and explore; however, the direction that is explored is often in an area where the true sense of the word cannot be found.

As I have shared in earlier segments of this book, purpose has nothing to do with what you do or a type of physical action. Remember, the true essence of purpose comes from the soul, while actions and positions have everything to do with this physical reality. The spiritual realm casts the manifestations of the physical realm. By this, I mean whatever occurs in that place will manifest in this physical reality.

If I shine a light on an object and it casts a shadow on the wall, it appears as if the action is taking place on the wall. This is not the case; the projection is causing the perception of what is real. This is how purpose works. We see people accomplishing great things, becoming business owners, doctors, graduating from school, taking on vocations like teaching, writing, etc. But all of these accomplishments are shadows on the wall. The actual actions of human beings are byproducts of the soul.

When we do things in order to add purpose to our lives, we never seem to find what we were looking for in the first place. It can be compared to studying the shadows on the wall. This is the real reason why so many people struggle in this area. This is why so many people are unable to find their purpose. It cannot be found, because most people are trying to examine the shadows on the wall and not the actual object that creates the shadow.

Purpose is about the soul. I am so happy for you because you have prepared yourself to find what your purpose is, if you are still unaware as to what it can be. The first step to finding purpose is the process of being re-centered. This occurs when one is led by their soul and not their mind. You have done this; therefore, you are closer to it than you realize. By becoming re-centered, you are now allowing your focus to leave the shadows on the wall and you are now dealing directly with the object that makes the shadows.

Purpose has nothing to do with what you do or what position you hold; it has everything to do with being.

Purpose has to do with your consciousness and awareness. When you allow yourself to respond to the energies and guidance of your soul, you automatically become authentic to your individual journey. When your focus is on "being," the "doing" part becomes quite easy.

Have you ever seen people who try things and always fail at them? Every time they do something, it never works and they continually work themselves into deeper states of frustration. Have you ever seen people who seem as if they are cursed or have continuous bad luck? This occurs because the person is not living in a state of authenticity. When I become re-centered and authentic, my path is made for me. I begin to pursue things I was made to pursue. The people around me are already planted in those positions; it's as if the map has been laid out for me.

It's not that the road becomes easy, but that the course has been plotted. Time and energy are not being wasted. You walk with a sense of certainty and confidence. Ideas come from all places and all directions. When you are participating in things that bring forth fruit, you do not become frustrated. You become motivated by the fact that what you have done is making a difference. Things are working for you because of your authenticity. Your focus is on being and not doing. When you become authentic, you act and live in authenticity. All of your needs are met and resources that you never knew you could obtain are within reach. So what's happening?

In the higher dimensions of reality, energy currents are coming together. In ancient times, there was a story of a great sword Excalibur, which was planted in stone. The sword had magical powers and would allow the person who could pull it from the rock to tap into those powers. Many people heard of this legend and traveled from far and near to attempt to free it, but legend said only a true king would be able to pull the mighty sword from the stone. One day, young Arthur crossed the path of the mighty Excalibur; he clenched both hands around it and pulled with all his might. For the first time in ages, the sword came up from the stone and its powers were released into the hands of Arthur. The young man eventually became one of the most famous kings of Britain. He would rule Britain's Camelot.

All of us, metaphorically speaking, have an Excalibur that is set in stone. Our Excalibur is not located in this dimension, but rather in a dimension above our reality. There is only one person who is able to remove Excalibur from the stone and that is you, when you find your purpose by way of re-centering your consciousness. When your focus revolves around being and not doing, that sword is released from the stone and energies of that dimension are released.

The power and energy of you finding your place releases something in the atmosphere that you can feel and experience. People will appear in your life, providing you with information that you need; before, you never understood where to look for it. Thoughts will come into your consciousness that help to make your journey more impactful. Enemies and people who are made to remove you from your path will turn into your greatest assets. Things will work, because there is a power unleashed in higher dimensions when you find your Excalibur.

Years ago, I was disappointed in my journey. I was experiencing waves of success; however, a true sense of fulfillment was just not there. I finished college and went on to pursue my Masters' degree. I even spent almost five years working on my doctorate. After all of those accomplishments, I felt as if I had done nothing.

One day I got on my knees; I prayed and I meditated on my situation. I decided at that point that the rest of my days would be different. No longer would I focus on doing, but being. I went through the same process of re-centering that I have shared with you. When I knew I was ready to change and make the transition in my life, I did. I gave up many things and I turned away from many people. I went through all that I have shared with you. I have never shared what I am about to write with any other person before this point.

After I made the transition which occurred over a period of six months, I fully surrendered myself to my authentic purpose. I prayed a prayer that I will never forget. It was the most powerful prayer I have ever prayed. After I cleaned my life and totally re-centered myself, I fell upon my knees and said, "Lord, I am ready." I didn't know what I was ready for, but I knew that I was and I knew something had changed.

The same week, my father was preparing to release a gospel album. I was excited because I had the opportunity to sing with him on the recording. Dad is an ol' pro, but this was my first time. I was so happy because I knew it would be something I would never forget. My dad is my hero and I learn so much from him. Not only is he my hero, but he is a hero to so many others. I am blessed and privileged to be his son.

At the end of that week, my dad took time to secure the team of individuals who would be working on his album. The team consisted of a marketing person, a radio person, a PR expert and a type of lead or point person for the project. He got up one night and told people, "I am not doing this album for money, my legacy or for myself. I am doing this album because I want its successes to be the foundation that allows my son to go higher than I did." Boy was that touching! I wanted to cry like a baby, but I couldn't break down at that time.

When the team was assembled, we prepared to travel to Cincinnati for the first public release of the album. All of the team members were there. While we were all there, I met the young lady who was responsible for the marketing. I had seen her in passing a few times but I knew nothing about her and she knew nothing about me. After things ended that night, my father and I had some time together in private. We were just talking, as we always do, when out of nowhere, he told me, "Son, I think she is the person you need to assist you with the things that I know you want to do. Your ministry is different from mine; you have a lot of gifts and talents and I believe she can assist you in your efforts."

What?! Dad had no clue of what I had prayed for. What was going on?

When I re-centered myself and removed my Excalibur, power in the higher dimension was released. The person who was made to do what only I was made to do had found his purpose. I had found my purpose without doing anything, it all revolved around being. The next week, my father told the young woman what he wanted her to do and that's when the ball began to roll for me.

At our first meeting, I shared with her all that I wanted to accomplish. All the other times I had shared this with people, they told me I was crazy and weird. I had heard that so much that I began to believe it, so I never said anything else to anyone. I just went with the flow, even though I knew "the flow" wasn't my path. When I shared with her what I did, she completely understood and loved everything I wanted to do. Not only did she like it, she was able to fill in the blanks that I had no answers for.

Are you serious?!! This couldn't be happening. It was as if I was dreaming! This person seemed to know my very thoughts and I knew hers. What in the world could be happening? Again, when you find your Excalibur, those energies are released. All types of spiritual ammunition come in your life in ways that you have never dreamed. I knew this was right, because I could feel it was right.

I had changed my entire life and taken the time to re-center myself. As soon as I did that, my life changed and I became a different person. As we continued working together on this one-off ministry plan that people had never seen before, we begin to unveil things as they came. A radio show, live events, ministerial opportunities, national radio shows, blogs and websites; you name it and it was done. Every single thing that was done was an instant success! Nothing failed, nothing was squandered, nothing was anything other than perfect!

This has nothing to do with my gifts and talents, but my purpose. It's about filling the space you have created with things that are birthed from authenticity. Purpose cannot be about a title, job, or a particular event. All of those things stem from your sense of consciousness or being.

When Arthur removed Excalibur from the stone, he was presented with a different life. There were things inside of him that were presented to him. Abilities and talents were suddenly manifested when he found this Excalibur. Arthur's life was changed when he found this mighty sword that was made for him. When you discover your purpose through authentic being, your life changes. Higher dimensions of reality began to shift and change, causing shifts and changes in this physical reality. Remember, the physical reality that we live in is nothing more than the projection of a higher dimension.

So here I was, six months into this new journey. In the process of being authentic, I was able to extend opportunities for others to share in this party. The challenges that you see at the end of each chapter were birthed from many of the ministerial exercises I have done with other people. It was a unique way to cause people to refocus their thoughts on the edification of others. A spirit of giving and generosity must be ingrained within people; this was a way for me to do that.

On one occasion, I asked people to submit suggestions, via online social networks, of how they would challenge other people. They had the freedom to do or say whatever they desired. We had a friendly competition to see the ideas people had. People submitted their ideas and we received challenges from all over the country. They piled in day after day. When all of the entries were submitted, we decided on two winners. The two winners had completely different challenges; however, they were both great. We scheduled a time for the both of them to film their challenge so that we could send the challenges out for all to participate.

The first winner contacted us and set up a time to come in and record the challenge. When she arrived at the studio, I had only seen her once before, at an event I'd hosted a few weeks prior. I did not know her and she did not know me. I knew nothing of her origin, educational background, vocation, or anything like that.

After we finished recording, she asked if she could set up a time to interview me. I asked what the interview would entail and she said she wanted my honest opinion on a few questions. Certainly! We met via phone conference. When the interview began, I had no clue what she was going to say, I just went with the flow.

She started asking me questions about writing, sharing a few statistics about books and writers that I did not know. She also wanted my thoughts and opinions on the actual interview, to help her refine the process in order to enhance her own marketable appeal. All while she was talking, all types of lights were going off in my head.

By the end of the interview, she asked me what I thought. If I were considering writing a book, she asked, would the series of questions and information shared be of interest?

"Absolutely!" I exclaimed.

The interview planted a seed in my spirit. I knew it was time for me to make a move and I had to do it then! When things shift in the higher dimensions, the energies produced will often times consume you. I could not sleep and I could not eat. My mind was focused on writing a book. What would I write? I didn't know. How would I have time to do it? No clue. What would I name it? None of these answers did I have at the time; all I possessed was a drive and passion to do it.

Before Arthur found Excalibur, he had no clue he was made to be a king. When he found Excalibur, the path to the impossible was made for him. This is what happened to me. At the time, writing a book was far from my plans and desires. I figured by the nature of my job, I would eventually do it. I have written several articles as well as my dissertation, which were all published, but none of these were a byproduct of my authentic desires. I only did that so I could graduate!

Something stirred in me. I contacted the director of my team to get her opinion on what had occurred. I set up a meeting in order that all of us could sit and talk about the details. After the meeting, I got the thumbs up that it was something that I needed to pursue. It was the missing link, per se. When I accepted this great task, I wanted to do something that made a difference. I didn't want to write a book for money, fame, and self-promotion—I didn't even want my picture on the front! I wanted to create something that would help others. I wanted something that would lead others to the light. I wanted to write something whereby my life and my experiences could be a support system for other people. So I accepted it and I moved forward with it.

As soon as I accepted this awesome challenge, the answers to all of my questions came to me in a matter of moments! The theme, title, chapters, and book outline, even the image on the cover of the book was given to me instantly! This is a direct function of the soul. Whenever something is given to you instantly, it is a function and an act of the soul. The soul is in direct communication with your consciousness when you become re-centered.

When the soul speaks, it speaks in flashes; it requires no process of thought or time. I didn't need any planning meetings or suggestions. I didn't need the opinions of others as to what I should write. I didn't need any feedback. I knew it was right and I did it. So here I am, writing a book. Here I am, just like Arthur: I wasn't expecting this, but I am doing it!

Here I am, a man who never got anything above a C in any creative writing class. I was never a writer or a thinker. I was never the kid with all A's. I was always the one that everyone thought would be a screw-up. I was the "bad kid," the one who made all the fuss and all the ruckus. Well, that may have been my past, but when I found my Excalibur and removed it from that stone the ball game changed! And now, you're holding part of my soul's purpose as you read these words.

Just as my ball game changed, so can yours! There is something waiting for you. You know it exists; you have just never been taught where to look for it. As you attempt to fill your space, use this numbered guide as a support system on this journey.

How to Fill the Empty Space

1.) The first step to finding purpose revolves around the process of being re-centered. The process of being re-centered is laid out in Chapters 1-6. This MUST be done. Without the successful completion of this process, discovering purpose is not impossible; however, it's highly unlikely. Think of it as finding the restroom in a foreign home you have never visited before, in the dead of night. Can you find it? Sure, it's possible; however, it will take you a long time, and you may never find it.

When you become re-centered, the soul is in direct communication with your consciousness. This is what eases the process and the clarity of the direction and guidance.

2.) Once you become re-centered, it's time to discover your purpose. This is now very easy, because your authentic self will come forth in the essence of your being. There is a key to finding purpose and I will tell you where it resides. Where there is passion, there is purpose! What things in your existence do you have a true passion for? Where does your heart reside? Whose struggles do you find yourself wanting to make lighter? Within your passions, you will always find purpose. They are one and the same; however, many people are not able to find them because so many other factors distort their ability to know and understand their authentic selves.

3.) Once you identify your passion, follow and chase that goal immediately. This is very important. Whenever your soul gives you direction, it's important to act on it immediately. It's important because there are so many other energies and powers that are connected to the drive that it gives you. Your response will in turn unlock other energies for your path. Had Arthur removed Excalibur from the stone, only to reflect on his actions, how would it have affected his future? Whenever you are given something, pursue it immediately. Pursue it with passion and determination. Allow the pursuit to be as though it's your very last. Put all that you have within into it. The more you chase it, the more other avenues will open for you. As you pursue it, you will always remain in a state of happiness, joy and peace. You will always remain in this state because the soul is residing in a place that it is able to recognize and understand. You will find this to be true as you pursue your goals and desires.

4.) As you pursue your passion and goals, pay close attention to how you change as an individual. You will change because your new posture of authenticity will unlock many hidden realities about your soul that you never knew you had. When we live without being who we were made to be, we are unhappy, ineffective and stagnant; however, when we become re-centered and discover what and who we are, things from within will bubble up out of us. You will amaze yourself at the gifts and talents you are now able to access. You will feel like a superhero that just discovered their powers.

Your IQ will increase, your productivity will double. Your work ethic will be abnormal to others. Your mind will think and reside in the future. Ideas and thoughts will jump into your head as if your mind was the only place they could exist. Answers to questions will become easy for you. Solutions to problems will be found in your sleep. As you walk, paths will be made clear for you. Favor and protection will be forever in and around you. You will find yourself immediately delivered from problems. You will notice disaster all around you but somehow and some way, you avoid it. You are being who you were made to be. You are on the path that God laid for you. You have found your way, and when your way is found, all things of God's kingdom become accessed by a thought, without any delay!

> 5. You will be a magnet of great and good things. People and opportunity will be drawn to you like honey attracts bees. Whenever you find yourself at a point or place where something is needed, it will be a matter of moments when the phone rings or a letter arrives and you find out you have what you need. People with certain gifts and talents will find you; you won't even have to look for them. Opportunities for you to present your passions and dreams will be presented to you; you will never even need to ask. Everything you do will succeed; even when it appears as a failure to others, you will be blessed as a result of it.

This is how the empty space is filled. The empty space is filled by the productivity of your authenticity. Sure, you can remain changed in order that you live your life free of personal issues, but why just settle for that? Chase those dreams that you have or find them if you do not know what they are. As you chase them, your productivity will fill that empty space. It will lead to the change of others in ways you will never imagine. Your life will have worth and value to it because it will edify the lives of many people.

Remember, you don't have to accomplish what I have mentioned by being like anyone else, just be you. Find your Excalibur that is tucked away in stone, and when you do, watch out because the world will change. I am excited for you; you have come a long way. There is so much in store for you. It's up to you to find it!

Challenge

Locate and Retrieve Your Excalibur

1.) What are your passions? What things in life are you most passionate about? Whatever they are, write them down in your journal.

2.) What are your gifts? What are you are naturally good at? Can you draw, are you a singer, are you super friendly, do you have a great personality? Whatever they are, write them down.

3.) How do your passions and your gifts coincide? How does one influence the other?

4.) Once you answer all of the above questions, think about how your passions and gifts can change others. After writing them down, find an opportunity to exercise what you have now come to know about yourself.

Chapter 9

Disciples of the Light

My purpose has been made clear to me. I must not keep what I have learned to myself. There are others who need to find the light, and I will live the rest of my days sharing with others what I have learned for myself. The darkness is no place for any soul. The beauty of life can only be found within the light. I will be a candle that shares its flame with those who desire light. The treasures I have received are so great and vast, I cannot help but share them with all who are willing to receive it.

Once as a child, I attended an unusual church service, held at night. All of the participants gathered together and candles were passed out. I vividly remember the moment the pastor gave instructions to turn off all the lights in the church. The room went pitch black. I couldn't even see my own hand waving directly in front of my face.

Once the lights were off, music began to softly play. The pastor told everyone to think of a person or a personal situation they had been experiencing, and to focus on it at this time. Moments later, a bright light flared from the podium. That single flame allowed me to see everything else in the room. I was amazed to see how this one small candle could dispel the darkness in such a vast room.

I was just astonished; at that moment, I learned the power of light. Darkness cannot affect light as the light affects the darkness. Here we were in complete darkness, and one small candle was able to illuminate the entire room. Conversely, it's impossible to see how darkness affects light. It can't be done. Darkness and light cannot exist at the same time!

If I was amazed at what I'd seen up to that point, it was nothing compared to what I saw next. The pastor walked down the stairs of the podium and lit the candle of another minister. The minister did the same, and the process repeated itself until every single candle in the church was lit. From one flame came an entire roomful of light. No electricity was needed. The light in the room made it appear as though it was midday!

What a sight! What an amazing observation I was able to glean that day. In the process of witnessing that room being filled with beautiful light, I noticed several lessons that I believe can be applied more broadly:

1.) One flame, shared freely, was able to ignite the lights of everyone who desired it.

2.) One light was able to eliminate all the darkness that once existed.

3.) The temperature of the room changed; the longer the candles burned, the more energy they gave off, and I could feel the difference as temperatures rose.

4.) There was a sense of unity in the room. It was obvious that people in the room had a sense of connection as a result of sharing the same flame. It caused everyone present to remain within a similar state of consciousness.

At this point of your journey, you have become similar to that pastor. Now you are a keeper and carrier of the light. You have taken the time to identify the problems, change your life, and commit to a new way of living. You live within a realm of purpose and now it's time to share that light with others.

Instilled within every creature that has ever been created is the desire to remake itself. Most times this is accomplished through reproduction. This urge is universal, from the smallest single-celled amoeba all the way to wild African elephants. All creatures have been created to recreate. This is what makes life possible. Mortal creatures have become immortal by their ability and desire to recreate themselves.

Although this book revolves around a type of spiritual journey, the process of spiritual reproduction is key to the overall fulfillment of your journey. Just like the pastor with that one burning flame, we must, as carriers of the light, find disciples of the light to share the process. When we show them how the light has changed us, we are able to change them as well as empower them to change others!

Finding Other Disciples of Light

Have you ever gone to a party or social event and saw a person you were unable to look away from the entire evening? They did nothing to encourage your attention; there was just something about them that attracted you. Perhaps it was their smile or their confident posture. Perhaps it was their presence or their ability to make others around them feel comfortable. Whatever it was, you were drawn to them.

The entire evening, your attention was fixed on them. Wherever they went, your eyes followed. The attraction wasn't sexual, but more of a magnetic pull that you couldn't resist. All you wanted was to find out more about them.

What's the point of this story? The person who was so special did absolutely nothing to cause an attraction. Something inside of them did all of the work. In other words, there is nothing you need to do in order to meet other disciples of the light. All you have to do is be yourself and in time, you will notice that others are drawn to your light.

It's important to understand a few things. In an earlier chapter, I shared with you how attractive and alluring the light can be. Remembering these points can make you more successful in your efforts.

1.) The individuals who are attracted to your light are not going to understand the foundation of their attraction. Many times, they will express their attraction to you in ways that you may not initially expect. Physical attraction, the desire to be around you, obsession or disproportionate concern with your life and things that you do in your personal time are just a few examples of what you might experience. You must remember, they are guided and attracted to you by something they do not understand. You must understand and prepare for this before it happens.

2.) Maintain high levels of sensitivity to these people. When they begin to display the signs that I have shared, it's important that you identify them immediately. When a child shows athletic promise, even at the junior high school level and younger, a good coach is able to recognize those signs. You must mimic the behaviors of this good coach. You must be alert to individuals who desire to be disciples of the light. The mere fact that they are drawn to you means they desire and want what you have; however, at this point of initial attraction, they are unable to explain or articulate that to you. Even if you explained it to them, they would not understand it.

3.) Once you become aware of these individuals, it's time to engage them. Remember, your objective is to influence future disciples of the light. The only way the darkness can be forever eradicated from this earth is if other disciples of the light contribute to that process. At this stage of the process, your number one objective should be to learn their story. What is their experience, what problems do they face, and what goals do they possess? You are not necessarily digging for answers, but just giving them the opportunity to share and express themselves. Within their story is the road map of their journey. You will often understand more about them than they do themselves.

Until this moment, they have lived their lives being led and influenced by their mind. In their stories, you will be able to pinpoint examples of this. They will seem so misguided and confused to you. When you listen to them, you will hear so many problems that, if given time and attention, would cease to trouble them. No matter how tempting it is to take on a posture of correcting them, please avoid it! This is critical at this stage. All you want to do is listen and give attention to them.

At this point, just be there for them. Your light will draw out their contaminants. When they are in your presence, they will naturally have a desire to cleanse and purge, which can be difficult to take. However, do all that you can to absorb their pain and frustration. Allow them the opportunity to talk freely with you, without judgment or condemnation of their actions. This is a very important part of the process. Look upon it as cleaning the wound before the stitches are applied. Their souls have been infected and they desire to return where they came from: love, joy and happiness. Your light is a reflection of their home and they are drawn to you because of that. This is such a critical point of the journey, because you are in the presence of a person who you were once exactly like!

4.) Be patient! This is perhaps the most difficult step to uphold. You will have a strong desire to save and change this person immediately, but when you act in this manner before its time, you ruin the opportunity for them to change! Remember, you cannot desire that they change more than they desire it for themselves. As long as your desire for change is greater than theirs, their transition will not be authentic. It will be imposed by you, which means it will be temporary. You want a person to be in it for the long run. You want a person to view this as a lifestyle change, and not a spiritual diet of sorts.

The way you remain patient is by allowing them to come and go as they please. When they desire to talk and share, be there to listen. You will experience times when they drift off and you don't see them or hear from them. Don't look for them or search them out. Just let them be; they will be just fine. When you are away from them, apply the techniques of thoughts and praying for them while you are apart.

When they are with you, they will desire your love and approval, and alter themselves to be accepted by you. They see your light, but they do not understand what it is, nor its power. They are not even aware of the fact that they want it for themselves. The light will cause them to change when they are in your presence. The light will cause them to tell you their deepest darkest secrets. The light will cause them to tell you things they have never shared with any other person. Many times, they will appear to be changed and different individuals when they are around you. Don't view this as a type of lie or as them misleading you; they are simply trying to reside in a similar spiritual state to yours. However, they are unaware as to how that can be done. Let them do this freely, without your criticism.

When you see them drifting back to people and activities you know are harmful to them, don't chastise them. Allow them the opportunity to go and live life as they see fit. The light will be as a magnet to them. It will continue to draw and pull upon them and they will many times be unaware of it. Because you have never condemned or judged them, your presence shall become a place of happiness and peace for them. You shall be a place of comfort that they can return to whenever they desire. The ultimate catalyst for these individuals' change will not be you; it will be their journey.

When I was 25 years old, a good friend of mine took me crab fishing off of the coast of Florida. I am a city slicker, born and raised in Atlanta, so whenever I had the opportunity to do things like camping, fishing or hunting I jumped at the opportunity. Early that summer morning, my friend drove us to the docks. He handed me boots, a towel and a long, strange-looking string.

I had expected a fishing rod; how was I supposed to know crabs are caught with a line and not a pole? When we got to the end of the wharf, he baited my line and demonstrated what I was to do. He took his line and threw it out into the water. I followed his lead and did the same. As soon as I threw my bait into the water, I got a tug. Being the inexperienced crab fisher I was, I acted as if a 20-foot marlin was on the end of my line. I pulled and tugged with all of my might! He lunged at me, telling me to stop immediately, and grabbed the line.

"The key to catching crabs is to let them to come to you," he told me. "When you pull on the line, they realize you are trying to catch them and they will release the bait." Wow, what a lesson!

When you find potential disciples of the light who are living in the darkness, any feeling that you are trying to change them will cause them to break and run. You must be a constant fixture in their lives, allowing your light alone to lure them to you. Keep them "on the line," but it's imperative that you do not pull too hard. When you do, it negatively impacts your ability to help them the way they need to be helped.

Understand the Draw of the Light

If you keep in mind the four points shared earlier in this chapter, you will be much more successful in your efforts. As time progresses and you maintain a presence in their lives, you will see them go through four different states of progression. It's important to understand these stages in order that you will know when they are ready!

Stage 1: Attraction

This is the state whereby the person becomes attracted and drawn to you. As stated earlier, they are unaware of what it is and why they view you as they do. Most times, these individuals are not spiritual people; therefore, they are commonly disconnected from the understanding and the possibilities of spiritual connectivity.

They are people who live almost solely within a physical reality. Their consciousness revolves around this physical world and everything that resides within their understanding of this world. This is key to understanding them. You view the world differently than they do; therefore, they will act and interpret things not of this world through the lenses of their limited understanding.

When I was child, I had a puppy who saw his reflection in a mirror for the first time. Upon first glance, he didn't know what to do. He looked at it and he barked and nipped at it. He didn't know what it was, so his inability to understand what he saw caused him to act erratically. When these individuals are drawn to your light, they view it like the puppy viewing his reflection for the first time. They don't understand it and that causes them to act in ways that may seem erratic and strange. Allow me to explain the extremes of their actions and some ways their attraction can manifest.

Initially, as I mentioned earlier, you will find people who are drawn to you. They are inquisitive and intrigued by you, what you do and even people you associate yourself with. These types of individuals will desire several things from you.

1.) They desire to be in your presence. Whenever they are with or around you, your presence makes them feel comfortable and safe. You become a recharge center for them. When they are with you, they are happy and engaged; they are unaware as to the reason; however, it is evident that it exists.

2. They desire to be a part of your life. They desire to do the things that you do, go the places that you go and often times they will desire to have and belong to your circle of associates, friends or even family members. This is a deeper desire to connect with you. They become captivated by your life and even many of the things that you do.

3. They will pattern themselves after you. They will desire to dress like you, eat the foods that you eat and even act and emulate things that you do or say. They become copycats of sorts, desiring to be just as you are.

These are just examples of how your light can have an effect on people. They behave just like the dog that saw his reflection—erratic. They are unable to explain what "it" is about you, they are just intrigued and drawn to it. It's important to understand these things in order to properly handle the situation when it arises.

It is also important to understand that your light can adversely affect people as well. When my puppy saw the reflection that he did not understand, he growled and barked at it. It wasn't that he didn't like his image. Far from it—he was intrigued. But his inability to understand what he saw frustrated him.

You will find that even in the attraction stage, some people who are drawn to your light may not treat you like they like or appreciate anything about you. These individuals will often act in this manner:

1.) Purposely trying to hurt you with their words and actions. You will have done absolutely nothing to them, yet they treat you as if you are their worst enemy. They go out of their way to cause you drama and pain. They will talk about you to others and create mischief that causes people to think negatively of you.

2.) These individuals can be very envious of you. They will attack and talk about the very things that most draws them to you. If you have a nice voice, they will tell others how horrible a singer you are. If you are wearing a nice outfit or suit, they will say how bad it looks on you. If you are in a position of power or influence, they will do all they can to discredit you in any and every way. You must understand that their actions, though manifesting in negative ways, originate in their attraction to your light. They find themselves as puppy dogs, barking at an image that they are too frustrated to understand.

Sometimes human behavior can be illogical and erratic. As children, how many times have you seen young boys pick on the girls that they like? It makes no sense; it is just another example of how human beings, absent the guidance of the soul, are unable to understand the essence of your light.

Stage 2: Expansion

The second stage occurs when the person who is attracted to your light becomes changed by it. In Chapter 3, titled "Discoveries of the Light," I told you that when we walk in the light, we will discover things about ourselves that we were unaware of. This is a characteristic of light. If you go into a dark room, you will probably bump into things. You will hit walls and trip over shoes on the floor. When you shine light in the same room, you are better able to navigate. This is characteristic of the light. It allows you to see where you are going, so you can better navigate your way through.

The light is what they are missing from their lives. They are not consciously aware of it; yet their soul leads them to yours. But the darkness in their lives prevents them from becoming re-centered, and blocks them from understanding what they feel as well as why their lives are the way they are.

When the word "expansion" is used, it means that their consciousness or awareness increases. Their expanded consciousness allows them the ability to see many of the errors and discrepancies that they hold within themselves. Many of these elements they do not yet understand; however, in order for change to begin, the root of the problems must first be made known.

When these individuals are first exposed to your light, they will notice your unusual ability to maintain a state of peace and happiness. This is a rarity, and something about you that is immediately seen and noticed. Your ability to smile, remain peaceful and always appear as if nothing changes for you amazes them. They will see that and be attracted to that. They will desire that for themselves and it will show them their inconsistencies.

The mere fact that you are able to reside in this state will motivate them to desire the same thing. They do not and will not understand that your ability to reside in the constant state of peace, love and happiness is a direct result of the changes you have made. They will assume it is just a part of your personality. Either way, they will realize that they are unable to maintain themselves in a peaceful loving state, and their consciousness will expand as a result of this knowledge.

Secondly, they will take note of your life and the things that are important to you. Most people in the world attach happiness and success to material things; however, you are not like that. After being re-centered, your view of life has dramatically changed. They will notice these things about you. They will notice you don't pay attention to money, clothes and things of this world, the way others do. They will see this and desire it for themselves.

Many times, their behavior will change simply as a result of you being who you are. Sometimes the change will come by them observing you. Pay attention, and you will see their habits change right before your eyes. They may not give up all of the things they were once doing; however, their participation in these activities will lessen. Maybe they remain the same basic person who you initially met, but you will notice an adjustment, or shift, in the things that they talk about. You will hear them make statements about the things that they need to change in their lives or perhaps even the ways they desire to be different or better. These changes are the result of the light!

The final common change you will notice is how they act when they are around you. This is important because it will teach you the power of the light. When these individuals are around you, they already know what you stand for and how you are. They are not able to understand it; however, they clearly see you are quite different. Your language, focus, desires, conversations and even your presence is very different from others around them. When they are around you, they will subconsciously adjust their behavior.

1.) Many of them will not speak in the same way when they are around you. Perhaps normally they use profane language and have common conversations; however, around you it's a different story. They will automatically adjust, refraining from harsh language and the like. It has nothing to do with you telling them how to talk or what not to say. They will merely have been influenced by your light.

2.) Other times, you will notice them hiding things from you. Don't be surprised that they try to shield you from the negative parts of their personalities. They may act and sometimes even convince you that they have changed, when in reality they are still the same. They will say, "You know I stopped drinking," or "I don't go to those parties like I once did," when in fact many times they will still indulge in these things! If you don't understand what is really going on, you will perceive this as them lying to you, but that is not the case!

They are telling you things that are untrue, but you must try to understand the reason. They tell you these things because it is truly their desire to be as they tell you they are. It is truly their desire to stop visiting those places. They tell you they have stopped because your light has shown them the areas of their life that need to be changed. They tell you these things, subconsciously feeling that it will make you accept and approve of them. When this happens, allow them to act as they do. Never stop loving them, just understand that your light is changing them!

This is how the light works. It changes things wherever it goes. Most who are able to witness your light will not understand it unless they are a carrier of the light as well; however, its effects are easy to see.

Stage 3: Resistance

In order to understand this stage, you must understand why some people are more attracted to your light than others. The individuals who are attracted to your light have a different type of spiritual filter than those who are not.

Once I traveled to Curacao, a Caribbean island east of Aruba. The island is truly a beautiful place, and I am so thankful for the opportunity to have traveled there. When I got off of the plane, I noticed the citizens of the island giving me strange looks. They stared and pointed, and several asked where I was from. I told them I was from Atlanta and they were all shocked! Everyone assumed I was native to the island.

After enough people approached me to ask if I were from the island, I had to know what it was that made them think I was from there. When I asked, they said I had features that were similar to theirs. Features like my eyes, facial hair and my skin tone were familiar to them. They saw something in me that they knew in themselves.

This is the foundation of others' attraction to your light. Although I am American-born, these islanders saw something in me that was similar to them. Those who are attracted to your light are able to see something in your spirit that is like theirs. In you, they see our shared origins of love, peace and joy! This is the foundation of who you are; having gone through the process of being re-centered, you have discovered this, but they have not. They recognize something, but they are ignorant as to what that something is.

These individuals have holes in their consciousness. They are looking for the light and many times when they are exposed to yours they respond to it because it seeps through those holes. They have been looking for something, but they are not aware that the light is what they are looking for. It is this unknown fact that allows them to respond to you as they do. After the first two stages, they will enter the phase I call "resistance."

This is a necessary part of the journey that we all experience at different levels. When a person has been exposed to your light by way of attraction and gains an expanded consciousness, the way the light exposes their issues and problems will many times cause them to resist to the change. You would think they would welcome those changes; however, you must remember what we learned in Chapter 5, "Between Two Worlds."

Just as my grandfather fought death for a time before his transition, people who desire the light may enter a state of resistance. They fight the light because it forces them to be something they are not familiar with. They do not know what to expect, nor do they understand what they are fighting. Sometimes the easiest response to the unknown is to run from it! When they run, let them go. Do not search them out, for if you do they may feel pressured. Keep them in your thoughts and prayers until they return.

I was out one day doing some shopping when I ran into a young man at the store. We had nothing in common, not close in age, polar opposites. We passed each other in the aisle, and though I usually have tunnel vision when I'm shopping, getting what I need and not really engaging with other people, I began chatting with the younger man. We exchanged contact information to stay in touch. I was much older than he was; however, he seemed to be drawn to me and I allowed our friendship to develop. I purposely never talked about anything that was spiritual or touched on God. We simply interacted as friends and I allowed that to be the foundation of our connection.

He and I never went anywhere or hung out in secular terms, but I allowed him to see me whenever he wanted to. I knew where he was in his growing understanding of spiritual principles, and I understood the fact that he was attracted to my light but unaware of it. I was able to see many things about his life that needed to be changed. I knew how to help him, but I never pushed our conversations. I only responded to questions about spirituality that he presented to me.

When he discovered that I was a pastor and had a passion for God, he never asked me anything about it. That was his way of resisting. He didn't want to hear any of that because he loved his life just the way it was. Seeing as he never asked me those questions, I never commented on any of those things. I knew where he was and understood that it wouldn't be long before he would come full circle.

One day, out of the clear blue sky, he called me begging for help. He needed guidance and I told him I would help, but he must follow my instructions. I told him his success depended upon his ability to spiritually change, and he was ready to do whatever it took to make the change!

This is what you want to wait for. This is your entry point. This is your pathway to changing a person forever! It's similar to the difference between a rookie running back and a pro. The rookie is full of health, strength and vitality. He wants to run as fast as he can as soon as he gets the ball. The veteran, on the other hand, has patience. He understands that the offensive line needs time to do their job. When he gets the ball, he strategically waits for the hole to develop. He holds back until that happens and when it does, he exploits it and takes the gap at full speed.

This is the gap. You must be patient and allow it to develop. Allow your light to be the lure that keeps them returning to your presence again and again. Even when they resist, they will return. When they return, you can actively pursue leading and guiding them to change.

Stage 4: Submission

After the first three stages have manifested in their life, they are ready for change. They will be open and receptive to everything that you say and tell them. It's important to have a plan of action. One of the worst things that can occur is to have a person who needs help, but you have nothing to give them. Just because you have been re-centered and changed doesn't mean you automatically know how to change someone else. There is a science to it. Every person needs to take a journey of spiritual change. The journey has steps that allow them to go through and experience this change. It is a guaranteed process that allows all persons to change.

The journey allows a person to find the wounds of their soul, heal from those wounds, become empowered and learn to be a leader, and it teaches them how to help others as well. The only way you can assist others with their journey is if you have experienced your own. At the end of the book, I will reveal how you can experience the journey. The process and information is all free. It is there to help you as well as others who want change! When a person goes through this process, they will become a disciple of the light. They will be released and will share that light with all others they encounter. The more carriers of the light there are, the more darkness will be eradicated from every point of our world.

Challenge

Now that you understand how attractive the light can be, write down all the times you have been attracted to the light of others or how many times others have been attracted to your light. It's important that you understand this because it will help you identify in future encounters those who can be potential disciples of the light. Allow the following questions to lead you to your answers.

1.) How many times in your life have you been attracted to the light of another person, now that you know and understand what it is? Write down as many examples as you can.

2.) How did that relationship change and affect your life? Were you able to grow from it? If so, how?

3.) Have you ever had an experience that was similar to the story that I shared with you? Have you ever known people to be drawn to you for no apparent reason? If so, how did you handle the situation? Were you able to see purpose and rise from your relationship with them?

Chapter 10

Not of This World

As I look at my reflection, I do not recognize what I see. I have never known myself to look like this. My appearance is different from those around me. I stand out; I glimmer while everything else around me remains flat. I am changed and I have become what I was made to be. Although I am different from everyone I see around me, I am glad I am who and what I am. My journey has not been easy and the road has been long, yet I am glad I have become the new creature that I am.

Once upon a time, long ago and far away, a creature by the name of Luxor lived in a place no human eyes had ever seen. Luxor had lived in this place for his entire life; he had never left because he never knew any other place but his home.

Luxor lived in darkness. Although he lived in darkness, he was not blind. Rather, the place where he lived was absent of light. Luxor had always resided in this place, and while he lived there he never knew that there was anything wrong with his home.

He got around just fine. He was able to live and eat; he hunted and gathered food. He even had fun resting and relaxing from time to time. Luxor enjoyed his life; there weren't any problems. The darkness was all that he knew; missing the light was never an issue because he had never experienced it.

The darkness affected Luxor's life in ways he was unaware of. The house that he lived in was made of straw and leaves. He rebuilt it often because the wind and rains caused his abode to deteriorate. His home would have been much more suitable had it been made of stone and wood; however, he never was able to retrieve those materials because the darkness kept him from finding them.

Luxor's diet was made up of fruit and various nuts. The fruit he ate was bitter to the taste. It sustained him, but it wasn't sweet. At the edge of his home where light shone upon the orchards were luscious apples and grapes, oranges and other exotic fruit. Had he known they were there, he would have retrieved them; but just like the wood and stone, he could not get them because the darkness kept him from knowing their location.

One day, Luxor was going on about his daily life and out of nowhere something exploded from the sky. He looked up and beheld something he had never seen positioned on the edge of the hill by his home. Living in darkness, Luxor had never before known the feeling of sight; this experience was highly unusual and very strange to him.

Luxor was seeing the light for the first time. He looked around at his home to see so many things he had never observed before. He saw the house that he'd made and how it was constructed from straw and leaves, then looked behind his home and saw trees and huge stones. He instantly realized that either would have made better building materials for his home, had he seen them when he was building.

He went into his home and saw the bowl of bitter fruit that was the staple of his diet. He threw it out, because on the other side of his home he saw luscious apples and grapes, oranges and other exotic fruits. He ran as fast as he could to reach and eat them; the sweet, bursting flavors brought him much pleasure.

Luxor stopped and he paused to look around at all he had never experienced. He then looked up at the light and knew this strange energy was what allowed him to experience all of these things. He stopped to reflect on this principle.

Without the light, an optimal living experience is impossible. The best choices are impossible to make because the darkness prevents those who reside within it from seeing and experiencing those things they need as well as those things that are best for them. If one continues to remain in the darkness, life will never have a true sense of meaning or purpose.

Luxor was so amazed at this new source that allowed him to see that he decided to follow it. He journeyed through the forests and over mountains. He traversed across deserts and he climbed over steep hills. The longer he journeyed, the brighter the light became.

Every path the light showed him, Luxor decided to follow. He learned so many things. There was a whole world he had never experienced. He saw fish and birds, huge trees and beautiful mountains. He reflected on his life before the light. All he had done on a day-to-day basis was to rebuild his house from the damage of the weather the day before, and gather bitter fruit. Now, he was experiencing things he never knew were possible.

Life had a new meaning to him; he had thoughts and visions of things that were never a part of his past. He had a desire to build things and to go to new places. He wondered about the places that he witnessed and how they came to be. He wondered about the light and what or who held it. His mind began to develop and open. Luxor never desired to eat bitter fruit or live in a house of straw and leaves again. All he wanted to do was follow the light. That energy changed his entire understanding of all things.

Before he made up his mind to follow the light, Luxor stopped and paused. He looked around at all of these new experiences that the light allowed him to see. He looked back over the darkness that he came from and reflected on this principle.

Whenever the light is followed, the life of the journeyer will forever change. Walking in the light will cause the person who walks to see new visions and experience new things. Walking in the light doesn't change what is there; however, it will change your experience of what is there. Your experiences will change because you are able to see life and live life with a new perspective.

Luxor marveled at his new experiences. He was forever freed from his previous life of darkness. For so long, he had lived without the light, but now he would do all that he could to remain in its presence. His life seemed so rich; he did all that he could to absorb every moment of the experience.

One day, Luxor stopped and looked around from the highest point of the land. He held up his hands to see strange patterns on his arm. It was scar tissue from an old, deep wound. When he saw the scar, he remembered when and how it happened. Many years before, while working and rebuilding his house in the dark, he fell upon a jagged rock. He'd felt the pain on that day, but had never, until now, seen its effects on his arm.

He then proceeded to look down at his feet. Years of walking the earth without seeing his path had affected his feet. Every time he'd taken a step, random objects cut his feet. Old scars and bruises covered his soles. He marveled at the damage that had been done.

Luxor hiked to a nearby stream, where he cleaned and washed the soles of his feet. Then he applied sage from a plant to help heal his torn soles. Luxor gathered materials from the forest and made coverings for his feet. For the rest of his days, he would walk with coverings upon the soles of his feet in order to protect them from the rough terrain.

Luxor anxiously wanted to see where the light would now lead him. Before he left his place of reflection, Luxor stopped and paused. He thought about how the light was showing him the effects of living in the darkness. He paused to reflect upon this principle:

Whenever one decides to walk in the light, the light will always reveal things that were previously unknown. The light will show how living in the darkness has caused pain and turmoil. It will allow the person who now walks in the light to realize its impact upon their life.

The light will also lead those who walk in it to a place of healing. They are shown the manifestations of pain caused by the darkness in order that they may address and ultimately fix it.

Luxor felt like a new creature. His feet were covered and he was able to move through the land at a high speed. He leaped, jumped and ran with a euphoric feeling of freedom and determination. The light was showing and revealing things he never imagined. What else would the light bring to him?

Now that Luxor was able to run freely through the land, it allowed him the ability to explore new areas. The path the light was making for him became a road that Luxor was tempted to deviate from. He found himself in the deepest parts of the forest, exploring lands he had never before imagined. He climbed atop trees to view the distant lands and terrain to come. He found himself resting, enjoying the endless breeze on the sides of the hills.

As time progressed, the light of the day that was endless began to slowly fade. His vision was leaving him as though the light was losing its power. Luxor panicked and became full of fear; he wondered what was happening and whether or not he would return to a state of darkness as he did before.

At the base of the hillside, Luxor saw the trail of the light as it dimmed in the horizon. All of a sudden, he jumped up and ran towards the light. He chased it down as though it was the last time he would ever see it. The faster he ran and the closer he got to the fading light, Luxor noticed that the day became full of light again.

The closer he got to its trail, the lighter the day became. Luxor had a revelation; at that moment, he learned that the reason light was cast upon everything that he could see was because he was following its trail. The light was leading him somewhere, and everything he saw was because the light had been guiding him along. He learned that the secret to never living in darkness was to always walk in the light.

Luxor promised himself that no matter how distracting his journey would be, he would always follow the light. As he ran to the light, vowing to never leave its path, he reflected on this principle.

There will always be things that lead us away from the light, but it is our job to keep focused. There will always be places that cause us to want to stop and rest; yet we must keep our determination and never stop. The light is what allows us to remain free from the darkness. The moment we stop following its path is the moment the darkness will return.

Luxor upheld the promise that he made with himself; he never again deviated from the path the light made for him. His journey continued to amaze him. . He heard sounds and interacted with creatures that left eternal impressions within his heart.

One day, as Luxor went about his journey, he came to a juncture; he seemed to be at the end of this land. The light had led him to a place that appeared to be the end of the earth. He was on the edge of a cliff overlooking a deep abyss of darkness.

The darkness frightened Luxor because he remembered how it had robbed him of so many things in the past. Luxor stood there, waiting and contemplating what to do. Here he was at the end of the land; he could not journey any further.

He wanted to turn around and reside in the beautiful landscapes his journey allowed him to see; however, he had made a promise to himself. He'd promised to never leave the presence of the light; he had promised himself that he would follow it. As Luxor stood looking into the deep abyss, the light continued to cut across its endless limits. As the light made its way across this mighty hole, hues of purple and deep blue were reflected in the path that the light had traveled. Luxor stared in amazement; it was as if the light had made a path for him in the midst of the darkness.

Luxor was torn. Though afraid of what lay beyond the veil of darkness, he knew the light was leading him that way. He wanted to reside in his land full of light and tress and beautiful landscapes. He wanted to stay and eat the wonderful fruits of the fields, and continue to feel the cool breeze of the evening upon his face, but as he waited there in turmoil the light began to journey away from him. The farther it went, the dimmer the light became to him.

Luxor looked back at his homeland, then turned to look forward in the direction of the light. He was torn, but he remembered the promise he had made with himself: "Luxor, always follow the light!"

Luxor took a deep breath, took five steps backwards, ran with all his might and when he got to the end of the cliff, he jumped! The longer he fell, the brighter his path became. While he was falling, Luxor thought about the place he left. In his mind, he reflected on this principle.

Sometimes the light will lead us to places that cause us discomfort. We are uncomfortable when we travel into areas of the unknown. It's important to trust the path that the light makes for the journeyer, even when we do not understand why it leads us as it does. Wherever it leads you, know and understand it will be the place that was made for you to reside in. You will desire to hold onto your past, not because it was better for you, but

simply because it is familiar. We hold on to those things because that familiarity causes us to feel as if we are in control. When I let go of the past to follow the light, my way will always be made for me, even if I am unable to see where I am going.

As Luxor continued to fall, the light continued to brighten his path. The brighter his path became, the more his descent slowed. It slowed until he softly landed upon a hillside. Luxor looked around and was surprised to see that it appeared to be the same place he left. He wondered about his new location; he was confused as to why the light would take him to the same place. Was this some sort of game? Some sort of test?

After the first few minutes of arrival, Luxor continued to look around a bit more closely. Gradually, he realized that while the place looked the same, he was seeing it from a new perspective.

Luxor was confused. The place was the same but it wasn't. He tried to force his mind to understand it. He recognized this hill because it was his native land; however, the appearance of everything was altered. Everything had a more dimensional look to it. Before, when he saw a flower or a tree it would be just that, a flower or a tree. But now when he looked at a plant, he was able to see its essence, almost like he was seeing its spirit. He could see the spirits of all living things now.

This essence hovered around all objects of this new world. It was as if Luxor was able to see the proof of life and how it sustained the object. In the old world, organisms appeared to sustain themselves, be it a tree or a bird or a fish, but now he was able to see this

mysterious energy that seemingly gave all things their
being.

things that move by force

Luxor explored the land and noticed this in all
things of this new world. All things, both inanimate
like mountains, rocks, and water as well as animate
objects like birds, fish and tree monkeys possessed
these auras. All things possessed a different color and
shape, too. He passed two trees of the same species;
however, the energy that hovered around one
appeared to be a different color and shape from the
other.

Luxor grew tired and dozed off, telling himself he
would explore the ends of this familiar yet strange
land when he awoke. Sometime later, Luxor rose and
looked around. To his shock, he was unable to see the
cloud of energy surrounding every object! What was
wrong? What happened?

Luxor thought perhaps he had dreamed it all. The
land looked just as he remembered it looking. The
trees, flowers and birds all looked like trees, flowers
and birds.

Luxor was confused and apprehensive. It had all
seemed so real the day before, but now he was in the
same old place. He looked around for the light to lead
him as it always did, but he saw no evidence of
anything. Luxor sat in disbelief and frustration. Had
the entire experience been a dream? It couldn't have
been. If it had all been a dream, why wasn't he living
in darkness? Luxor knew he wasn't dreaming, but he
had to understand why these strange events were
happening to him.

Luxor searched the land high and low, yet he found nothing out of place. He traveled deep into an old forest, lured on from a distance by something he had never seen before: ten huge mountain birds roosting in the densest, thickest part of the forest. It was a strange sight. Mountain birds didn't belong in the jungle. They hovered above him as though they knew him and even why he was there.

Luxor gazed at them and they gazed back to him; then they took flight and Luxor ran to follow them. He instinctively felt that they were leading him somewhere, but he didn't know what for. As he climbed over hills and jumped the crevasses of the forest, something thundered overhead.

It was a roar like no other, and as he looked up it seemed the birds were leading him toward the source of this noise. The closer they came, the louder the noise grew. Finally, Luxor came to a mountain. The birds never left him, but hovered patiently, so he began to climb the side. The mountain birds stayed in range the entire way up the mountain. When Luxor got to the top, he beheld something he had never seen.

A giant waterfall of sorts poured out energy onto the entire land. This energy appeared to be the same substance that surrounded every living thing the day before. It was bursting with beautiful metallic flakes of purple and hues of gold and silver. It was its own unique color that his eyes had never seen.

Luxor gazed in amazement and walked closer to this fall. He stood under it and raised his hands, held back his head and became one with this fall. He could feel no pressure caused by this mysterious fall, but he felt something going into his body. The moment he immersed himself, he experienced a surge of pure, unrefined energy that filled him from his feet to his head.

When Luxor stood underneath the fall, his eyes closed, but now he slowly opened his eyes. He realized he was not dreaming. As he looked around, he was able to see the energy and essence of all things; however, this time they were bigger and more robust in his sight! Not only did he see these energy fields, he was able to see that they all came from this fall. This fall was the source of all things. When he became one with it, it became one with him. Luxor gazed in amazement, then stopped and paused... He reflected upon this principle.

There is a source from whence all things come. The light is what leads us to it. The light is from the source; however, it's the source that gives us our being. Connection with the source is what creates a different experience of all things. The source doesn't adjust the circumstance of the observer; however, it does allow the observer to see things that are beyond the physical reality. The more the connection between the source and the observer is nurtured, the more the observer is able to see things for what they are instead of what they appear to be.

Luxor decided to make the mouth of the fall his sanctuary. Before the start of each day, as well as at the end, he submerged himself in the fall. It filled him and satisfied his being. The more he connected with the fall, the more he was able to observe and see in the land.

Luxor existed in a realm that was above what he once saw. He took his time roaming around the land experiencing this higher dimensional experience. The land that he once thought he knew held new insights for him. He was able to understand how all things were sustained by the source energy that came from this fall.

As he walked throughout the land, Luxor found himself drawn to certain parts of it. He really didn't know why, but something besides his own desires was leading him. One day he journeyed to the very edge of the forest that contained the fall; and there he heard a disturbing commotion. He looked and saw a jungle beast chasing a smaller field rodent.

The way the larger animal hunted the smaller one, Luxor knew the smaller animal was in trouble. As the predator closed in on the rodent, he lunged out, devouring it in one clean experienced motion. The field rodent was literally there one moment and gone the next. As Luxor looked upon this scene, he saw not only two animals in their physical bodies, but their higher dimensional beings as well—the energy shields worn by all things in the land.

As the jungle beast ate the rodent, the energy cloud that surrounded the smaller animal merged with that of the larger one. The color, shape and size of the jungle beast's energy cloud changed before Luxor's eyes.

It was as if the essence of life continued even after the animal no longer lived. Luxor learned that the source that powers all things sustains life with an energy that can never be destroyed. The jungle beast changed in this higher dimension; yet it looked the same in its physical body. Luxor left this scene with a greater understanding of the new world he found himself in.

As he traveled on, he continued to notice the power fields surrounding all things. Though everything had a different color or variation to its color tone or sequence, all were shades of purple, silver and gold, the colors of the energy fall atop that mountain. . It was as if the fall was the whole and all other things were tiny parts of it. This amazed Luxor.

He came across a small animal that was very birdlike. From a distance, Luxor watched it sitting calmly beside a pond. For some reason he was drawn to it; however, he did not know or understand why. As he approached it, he sat and extended his hand to it. He had a sense of familiarity with this creature, but he didn't understand why he felt that way.

The animal hopped gently onto his hand. Luxor closed his eyes and when he did, he was taken back to the days he lived in darkness. Whenever he would journey outside his home, for straw to repair some part, he would play with a creature similar to this small bird. It always brought him joy and excitement. The times when he interacted with the bird were special to him. He had never laid eyes on the animal, but now he understood that this was the same creature.

A pure, clean feeling exuded from him. Luxor did not understand it, but it made him feel something special for this creature. He cherished it and had a deep connection to it. This creature was the only thing that brought him a sense of joy when he lived in the darkness.

Leading others to the light

Holding the bird, filled with this strange feeling, reminded him of standing beneath the great fall. When the energy of the fall filled him, the feeling was similar to how he felt holding this creature. When he opened his eyes, Luxor noticed something happening in his energy cloud. Some of it left him and became a part of this creature. He saw the same colors and hues of the fall. Luxor had transferred some energy from himself to this creature. He sat there in complete amazement.

Luxor stopped and paused to reflect on this principle.

Once connection to the source is made, a different understanding of all things is established. The observer will see that all things are sustained from this one source. When this is understood, the experience of life will change. Connection to the source is the most important element of the observer's experiences. Without it, life is absent of understanding. With it, life is full of joy, happiness, peace, love and guidance.

Luxor interacted with every creature and living thing he could, as often as he could. This became the foundation of his existence. Each day and night, he'd return to submerge himself under the great fall. It always felt like the very first time. Eventually, Luxor had a nagging feeling that something was missing from his existence. He felt as if something needed to be done, but he did not know what it was.

One day after leaving the fall, Luxor had a sense of understanding as it related to his journey. He knew the rest of his time in this new world should not be spent filling himself. His purpose was to share what had filled him, so that others could be filled as well.

Luxor knew this with all of his heart. The revelation came to him in a flash; he knew exactly what he was to do. He said to himself, "I must go now and help others who are like me. The light led me out of darkness; the light led me to the source. I was filled with its great power and now I must share with others what I have come to know!"

Luxor stopped and paused to reflect on this principle.

When the observer connects to the source, purpose and direction in life are given and understood. The only way purpose can be understood is when connection to the source is made. Once connected to the source, the observer becomes connected to a higher power and gains understanding of a dimension that is above the physical. Purpose cannot be understood by the mind; instead, it is inspired by the soul. The power of the source is what allows this to occur.

When purpose is given, its totality is never fully revealed. The observer is led, and during that experience all things needed to fulfill that purpose are given. The walk becomes one of faith and not sight. All things are understood, not based on what is seen or heard, but rather what is felt in the soul.

Luxor ran with all his might in a new direction. He didn't know who he was to assist or even where he was to go, he just knew his life had a purpose that was greater than anything else. He knew his experiences were designed for others and not just himself.

Luxor began to journey in a direction he had never expected to go. He headed toward his old home! He was returning to the land of darkness. Luxor had to do all that he could to share what he had been given. He had to share the light that led him out of darkness.

Luxor's journey was long and difficult, and he found himself missing the time spent submerged under the great fall. He grew weak, yet he continued on his path. Luxor journeyed over hills, mountains and across the seas. He knew he was close.

The closer Luxor came to his village, the weaker he became. He recognized the land and could tell he was quite close. There was a sphere of sorts that surrounded the land of darkness. There was a clear separation between the darkness and the light. He knew this because of his abilities to see beyond the realm of the physical.

The land of darkness was in a large valley; it appeared to him as a deep hole within the land. Luxor pressed on with all of his might. He was so sick and devoid of the power he once possessed, when he approached the mouth of the land of darkness he could barely stand. It was as if the darkness was stripping him of all of his energy. Luxor knew this was no longer his home, but he had to do all he could to help those in his native land.

When he looked into the valley where he came from, he was shocked. He gazed at the scene again, aghast. Hundreds of thousands of creatures were living there in darkness. They were pale, colorless; their skin looked transparent and thin. Their bodies were bent to the ground, unable to stand straight. Their hair was matted and full of dirt.

As Luxor observed them, he looked for the essence of their being and noticed something very strange. Around their bodies was nothing. These creatures had nothing like the aura that surrounded the carriers of the light. They existed within their own dark world, naked and weak. Luxor knew he was once just like them, and his heart was saddened.

Luxor was so weak. The absence of energy left him unable to move or do anything other than look and observe. As he continued to study people, he saw that all of them were involved in the same activity: building up their homes. They couldn't see where they were going, but it was obvious this was routine for them.

They were building their homes up just as he once had, using the same materials of mud and straw. Luxor watched them each day, rebuilding houses that were damaged by the wind and rains of the previous day. Luxor was watching himself; this is where he came from.

He saw they all ate the same bitter fruit he used to. They were trapped in the darkness just as he had been trapped. Luxor had to save them, but how? He wanted to go into the land and pull them out one by one, but he could not journey any closer to the darkness. He had been changed and no longer had the ability to move within that realm. They would never see him. The only way they would be able to leave the land of darkness was if they too, saw the light that had led him out.

Luxor was far from the fall, weak and unable to journey back to recharge his strength. How could he help them in this state? Luxor sat on the edge of the valley and turned his focus inward. He connected to the infinite source that gives life and power to all things. Immediately, he felt his power return. His strength and prowess increased. He felt as if he were a brand new creature.

Luxor had learned a valuable lesson. Previously, he'd bound the power of the source to a specific place and location. He assumed that unless he was in that place, he could not connect with the source. He learned that the source transcends space and time. It is always within. He could connect with it whenever he desired. His thoughts allowed him to be filled far away from it, just as if he were directly under it.

As Luxor connected with the supreme source, he turned around atop the hillside of the land of darkness. With his hands lifted and his head back, he absorbed the energy of the source. All of a sudden, the inhabitants of the land of darkness looked up. To them all they saw was light, but it was Luxor who allowed the light to be shown to all who were in that valley.

The inhabitants of the land looked around in amazement. Suddenly, they were able to see what had been hidden from them by the darkness. Luxor stood watching many of them respond just as he had. They pointed at the wood and stones. Luxor knew they were marveling at how much stronger their homes would be if they used them instead of straw and mud.

They looked upon the hilltops to see the luscious grapes, oranges and other exotic fruits and threw out the bowls of bitter fruit. They examined each other's bodies, looking at the various cuts and bruises caused by their life in the darkness. The light brought them much understanding about their past.

Time passed, and Luxor noticed something that concerned him. All of his people remained where they were. They stayed right there in the land. They changed the materials used to build their homes, ate sweet fruit and cared for their wounds caused by the darkness, but none of them left. Luxor was saddened. He stopped and paused to reflect upon this principle.

Just because an observer is exposed to the light, doesn't mean they will follow it. There are times when the observer will be satisfied with what the light has done to temporarily eradicate the darkness. In order for the person to live in the fullness of their existence, the light must be followed and not just observed from a distance. Only when it is constantly followed, can the person find their way to the source.

Luxor was deeply saddened; he turned away from this valley to return back to his sanctuary. Luxor felt as though he had failed his people. He had shown them the light, but its effects would only be temporary. Luxor knew that it was only a matter of time before they returned to the state they were in before he came. As he walked away on his journey back to his home, he turned around and to his surprise he saw someone had followed him.

Luxor was elated! An inhabitant of the land of darkness followed him from the valley. He turned and ran toward the creature, but when he approached him, the creature seemed to look straight through him. Yet, as Luxor moved, the creature moved as well. Luxor then realized that, although the creature was unable to see him in his body, he was still following his light.

Understanding dawned on Luxor. This creature was unable to understand what he was seeing because Luxor and the creature existed in two different dimensions! It all made sense. Luxor headed back towards the source, the endless fall of energy! He knew it was his job to lead the creature to the source, just as he was led to it. Luxor appeared to this creature as light, and although all of the other inhabitants were in the valley, he was happy that one decided to follow him!

Luxor did not retrace his steps to lead the way to the source. Instead, he returned to the source the way he had first approached it. He led the creature through the valleys and up the mountains. He led him over the dessert plains and through the cavernous hills. Every place he moved, the creature followed, just as he had.

Luxor continued until he led the creature to the end of the earth. The creature stood on the edge of the hill, uncertain about leaving his native home. The creature looked behind him and in front of him. As he waited, the creature could see the light fading away. He braced himself, took a few steps backward, then ran and jumped.

When the creature leaped, Luxor's task was complete. It was now up to the creature to find his way. Luxor watched him from a distance. He knew this was something his friend had to complete on his own.

The creature navigated through the thick trees of the jungle, coming to a place where he was unable to move further. The new creature stood wondering where to turn and where to go. A tree monkey sat near the creature; Luxor closed his eyes and focused. He connected with the essence of the tree monkey just as he had with the source.

Luxor led the monkey to the new creature just as the birds were led to him. The tree monkey jumped from limb to limb and the new creature followed on foot, knowing the monkey was guiding him to a particular destination. The new creature climbed the side of the mountain and when he arrived at the top, he stopped and gazed in awe.

He saw a giant fall that washed a gorgeous substance over the entire land. This fall of energy appeared to be the same substance that surrounded the plants and animals he had witnessed along the way. It was bursting with beautiful metallic flakes of purple and hues of gold and silver. It was its own unique color that his eyes had never seen.

The new creature walked up to the fall and allowed it to flow all over him. He closed his eyes, threw back his head and raised his hands. He stood for several moments, totally consumed by this mighty fall of pure energy. Luxor gazed at him, happy that the new creature would be able to see him now because they resided in the same dimension. Still, Luxor did not interrupt him underneath the fall, because he knew it was a special time for this new creature.

Before Luxor's eyes, this creature began to change, and Luxor was amazed at what he saw. The pale, translucent skin turned a beautiful combination of colors. His hair became long locks of strength and power. His countenance and posture was made erect, tall and straight. His shoulders broadened as if a potter had sculpted them. Luxor knew that he, too, had undergone this transformation. He was able to see himself in the new creature.

The new creature turned around slowly, facing Luxor for the first time. Two beings from the same place, changed because they followed the light.

When the new creature turned around, it was as if he already knew Luxor was standing there. He had no look of surprise, only expectation. Luxor gazed into his eyes, marveling at the beautiful multi-colors that were shown on his cheeks. He gazed into his large flame-like eyes. His locks flowed in the wind. Luxor looked at this creature and placed his hand upon his shoulder.

He said, "Chomar, my name is Luxor. Go now and return to the land of darkness. Share your light with all who reside there. Allow your light to shine upon that hill. Whosoever has the will or desire to follow it, be the light that guides them on their journey. It's not your responsibility to tell them what to do. Just allow your light to shine and someone will follow."

Chomar looked intensely into eyes that looked like his. "My brother," he said, "please journey with me and help me to deliver more of our people from the land of darkness."

"I cannot go with you; I am not of this world," Luxor responded. "This place is not my home. I have finished my task. Go now, Chomar, and cast your light on the land of darkness. I will see you again."

For the balance of eternity, one by one, the inhabitants of the land of darkness were led from the prisons of pain and despair. As Chomar turned to begin his journey to the land of darkness, he paused to reflect on this principle.

Every person who lives should desire to follow the light. Had Luxor not been willing to follow the light, he never would have made it out of the darkness. Our willingness to follow the light will lead not only ourselves from the darkness but also others. All things that exist are meant to procreate. When the light is found, take it and share it with someone else. If we all follow the light, and see to it that others receive the light, the world and all parts of it will forever be outside of the presence of darkness.

THE END

Where Are You On Your Journey?
Ways to stay connected...

Life a journey; it is a collection of events and earthly experiences that take us from where we start to where we finish. The hope of each journeyer is to learn from every experience while being on that journey.

Not of This World is a book that takes the reader on a journey. The journey consists of four stages of change: **Healing, Transformation, Empowerment and Expansion.** The way I share my story as well as organize the contents of the book follows the format of these four stages.

When Luxor began his walk he started in the darkness, then he moved into the light, he next learned while being in the light; finally he led others to the light. As you can see, the process from start to finish follows this format: Healing, Transformation, Empowerment and Expansion.

I was inspired to take the contents and format of this book to organize and develop what is called, "The Journey." **"The Journey"** is

- **Specialized classes**
- **Small group sessions**
- **Individual assessments**
- **Personal life coaching and mentoring**

This program and its services are designed to take any person with any problem at any point of his or her life from where they are to where they need to be.

"The Journey" will become the foundation program of my personal non-profit 501-(C)3 under the title and caption of "The Joseph L. Williams Foundation." It is my desire to partner with the public school systems, prisons, churches and communities in order to offer this wonderful program for people who desire to change!

If you have enjoyed the contents of this book and want to interact with me personally to be a part of "The Journey," visit us at www.jlwlive.com or facebook.com/truthknowledgelight. If you have any questions in reference to "The Journey" or questions or comments on *Not of This World* please email us at info@jlwlive.com.

Blessings!

JLW

About the Author

The quest for knowledge, understanding and personal development has always been a priority in the life of Dr. Joseph L. Williams. He is a graduate of one of the nation's top private schools, Woodward Academy in College Park, Georgia. He received his BA in Business from Morehouse College, Master of Divinity from McAfee School of Theology and Doctorate of Homiletics with a concentration in Classical Rhetoric from Mercer University in Atlanta.

Dr. Williams' training has led him to become eccentric in his thoughts, profound in his commentary and creative in his unique style of authorship. Indeed there is a new nation of young storytellers on the rise and Dr. Joseph L. Williams is one who will make great contributions to the improvement, progression and edification of modern day society.

Our society exists within a comprehensive consciousness of fear and doubt; substantive writing that lends itself to the personal change of people is indeed a missing component. Future projects from this young author will serve as the impetus that will move society from the present to the future.

If you are interested in booking Dr. Williams for speaking engagements or appearances, contact info@jlwlive.com

CPSIA information can be obtained at www.ICGtesting.com
Printed in the USA
LVOW01s0326161013

357139LV00006B/50/P